MR 26 '03	DATE DUE		

OUT OF CONTROL

Gambling and Other Impulse-Control Disorders

■ **Am I Okay?**
Psychological Testing and What Those Tests Mean

■ **Anorexia Nervosa:**
Starving for Attention

■ **Child Abuse and Neglect:**
Examining the Psychological Components

■ **Conduct Unbecoming:**
Hyperactivity, Attention Deficit, and Disruptive Behavior Disorders

■ **Cutting the Pain Away:**
Understanding Self-Mutilation

■ **Disorders First Diagnosed in Childhood**

■ **Drowning Our Sorrows:**
Psychological Effects of Alcohol Abuse

■ **Life Out of Focus:**
Alzheimer's Disease and Related Disorders

■ **The Mental Effects of Heroin**

■ **Mental Illness and Its Effects on School and Work Environments**

■ **Out of Control:**
Gambling and Other Impulse-Control Disorders

■ **Personality Disorders**

■ **Psychological Disorders Related to Designer Drugs**

■ **Psychological Effects of Cocaine and Crack Addiction**

■ **Schizophrenia:**
Losing Touch with Reality

■ **Sexual Disorders**

■ **Sibling Rivalry:**
Relational Problems Involving Brothers and Sisters

■ **Sleep Disorders**

■ **Smoke Screen:**
Psychological Disorders Related to Nicotine Use

■ **Strange Visions:**
Hallucinogen-Related Disorders

■ **Through a Glass Darkly:**
The Psychological Effects of Marijuana and Hashish

■ **The Tortured Mind:**
The Many Faces of Manic Depression

■ **Uneasy Lives:**
Understanding Anxiety Disorders

■ **When Families Fail:**
Psychological Disorders and Dysfunctional Families

■ **A World Upside Down and Backwards:**
Reading and Learning Disorders

THE ENCYCLOPEDIA OF PSYCHOLOGICAL DISORDERS

Senior Consulting Editor Carol C. Nadelson, M.D.
Consulting Editor Claire E. Reinburg

OUT OF CONTROL

Gambling and Other Impulse-Control Disorders

Linda Bayer

CHELSEA HOUSE PUBLISHERS

Philadelphia

The author wishes to dedicate this book to Mary Glynn, R.S.M., whose insight into the psychological sources of personality has been most instructive over the years. A teacher in the fullest sense of the word, Dr. Glynn has dedicated her ministry to healing at the level where religion, medicine, literature, and art intersect. Her depth and intensity are gifts to all whose lives she has touched.

The ENCYCLOPEDIA OF PSYCHOLOGICAL DISORDERS provides up-to-date information on the history of, causes and effects of, and treatment and therapies for problems affecting the human mind. The titles in this series are not intended to take the place of the professional advice of a psychiatrist or mental health care professional.

Chelsea House Publishers
Editor in Chief: Stephen Reginald
Production Manager: Pamela Loos
Art Director: Sara Davis
Director of Photography: Judy L. Hasday
Managing Editor: James D. Gallagher
Senior Production Editor: J. Christopher Higgins

Staff for GAMBLING AND OTHER IMPULSE-CONTROL DISORDERS
Prepared by P. M. Gordon Associates, Philadelphia
Picture Researcher: P. M. Gordon Associates
Associate Art Director: Takeshi Takahashi
Cover Designer: Emiliano Begnardi

The Chelsea House World Wide Web address is
http://www.chelseahouse.com

First Printing

9 8 7 6 5 4 3 2 1

Library of Congress Cataloging-in-Publication Data applied for
ISBN 0-7910-5313-X

CONTENTS

Introduction by Carol C. Nadelson, M.D.   6

Impulse-Control Disorders: An Overview   9

1   An Introduction to Impulsivity   11

2   Pathological Gambling   25

3   Kleptomania—The Compulsive Need to Steal   41

4   Pyromania—The Compulsive Need to Set Fires   53

5   Trichotillomania and Similar Problems   65

6   Intermittent Explosive Disorder   75

Appendix: For More Information   84

Bibliography   85

Further Reading   88

Glossary   89

Index   91

PSYCHOLOGICAL DISORDERS AND THEIR EFFECT

CAROL C. NADELSON, M.D.
PRESIDENT AND CHIEF EXECUTIVE OFFICER,
The American Psychiatric Press

There are a wide range of problems that are considered psychological disorders, including mental and emotional disorders, problems related to alcohol and drug abuse, and some diseases that cause both emotional and physical symptoms. Psychological disorders often begin in early childhood, but during adolescence we see a sharp increase in the number of people affected by these disorders. It has been estimated that about 20 percent of the U.S. population will have some form of mental disorder sometime during their lifetime. Some psychological disorders appear following severe stress or trauma. Others appear to occur more often in some families and may have a genetic or inherited component. Still other disorders do not seem to be connected to any cause we can yet identify. There has been a great deal of attention paid to learning about the causes and treatments of these disorders, and exciting new research has taught us a great deal in the past few decades.

The fact that many new and successful treatments are available makes it especially important that we reject old prejudices and outmoded ideas that consider mental disorders to be untreatable. If psychological problems are identified early, it is possible to prevent serious consequences. We should not keep these problems hidden or feel shame that we or a member of our family has a mental disorder. Some people believe that something they said or did caused a mental disorder. Some people think that these disorders are "only in your head" so that you could "snap out of it" if you made the effort. This type of thinking implies that a treatment is a matter of willpower or motivation. It is a terrible burden for someone who is suffering to be blamed for his or her misery, and often people with psychological disorders are not treated compassionately. We hope that the information in this book will teach you about various mental illnesses.

The problems covered in the volumes in the ENCYCLOPEDIA OF PSYCHOLOGICAL DISORDERS were selected because they are of particular importance to young adults, because they affect them directly or because they affect family and friends. There are individual volumes on reading disorders, attention deficit and disruptive behavior disorders, and dementia—all of these are related to our abilities to learn and integrate information from the world around us. There are books on drug abuse that provide useful information about the effects of these drugs and treatments that are available for those individuals who have drug problems. Some of the books concentrate on one of the most common mental disorders, depression. Others deal with eating disorders, which are dangerous illnesses that affect a large number of young adults, especially women.

Most of the public attention paid to these disorders arises from a particular incident involving a celebrity that awakens us to our own vulnerability to psychological problems. These incidents of celebrities or public figures revealing their own psychological problems can also enable us to think about what we can do to prevent and treat these types of problems.

We all act impulsively at times. This happy couple did not intend to go into the water when they set out on their walk. Such innocent impulsive acts are part of everyday life for most people.

IMPULSE-CONTROL DISORDERS: AN OVERVIEW

We are all impulsive at times, but for most of us impulsivity does not control our lives. If a person has an irresistible urge to do something on the spur of the moment, does that mean that he or she has an impulse-control disorder? If an individual gambles, sets fires, pulls out his or her hair, or explodes in fits of rage, does the person have poor impulse control? Can we distinguish between "normal" behaviors and *pathological* (abnormal) disorders? If so, who is usually afflicted with these conditions? How long do the disorders persist? Are they treatable? What are the legal consequences of such impulsive actions?

This volume of the ENCYCLOPEDIA OF PSYCHOLOGICAL DISORDERS addresses these and other questions, as it defines and explains the mental conditions known as impulse-control disorders. The fourth edition of the American Psychiatric Association's *Diagnostic and Statistical Manual of Mental Disorders (DSM-IV)* lists five disorders in this category: pathological gambling, kleptomania, pyromania, trichotillomania, and intermittent explosive disorder. In the chapters that follow, in-depth descriptions of these disorders distinguish each from "normal" behaviors and illustrate how each can limit and control a person's life.

Based on recent research and case studies, this book provides insight into the underlying genetic (biologically inherited) predisposition that may play a part in causing impulse-control disorders. Actual cases help give readers a clear understanding of the ongoing scientific research and allow us to examine the effectiveness of various treatments. Recent findings point to the strong likelihood that, in addition to environmental and emotional factors, a biochemical element may contribute to the pathological behavior that characterizes people with poor impulse control. In many cases, medication, in addition to other therapies, offers new hope to individuals afflicted with these disorders.

9

People with impulse-control disorders often share an underlying disappointment with life. The feeling that they have somehow been cheated out of their due can cause these individuals to lash out, as this man is doing, at those around them.

1

AN INTRODUCTION TO IMPULSIVITY

Denise is worried about her boyfriend, Don. In fact, she has threatened that, if he doesn't get his act together, she will end their relationship altogether. The only person he seems to care about is himself.

Don's track record with women isn't good. If Denise breaks up with him, she will be the fourth woman who has left him in the past three years. Don doesn't worry much about the women he's lost, though. In his mind, they all seem like the same person with different names. But he does enjoy the way Denise brings him food and cleans his apartment, so he's been working hard to manipulate her into staying with him a little longer.

Denise complains that Don is never on time for their dates, and he's unwilling to make plans with her for the future. He wants what he wants right now, and she feels that he behaves like a spoiled, impatient child. She knows that Don's childhood was difficult. She also understands that, deep down inside, Don is fearful that he doesn't measure up to other people's expectations. Denise feels sorry for him, but at the same time she wonders whether Don is capable of maintaining a mature relationship.

The final straw for Denise comes when she discovers that the money Don has reputedly borrowed from her has all gone to pay for bets at the racetrack. When Denise confronts Don about his gambling, she learns that he owes money to just about everybody he knows. He has been gambling for years, and he just can't seem to stop himself. Denise knows that he needs help. In fact, Don may have one of the mental disorders that psychologists refer to as "poor impulse control."

The word *impulse* refers to a seemingly irresistible urge to do something on the spur of the moment. When an individual acts on impulse, he or she has not considered the alternatives to or the consequences of the behavior. Impulsive individuals such as Don may often act on a whim. Researchers are not certain whether this trait is inherited genetically, created by environmental factors, or a combination of the two. For example, some people with poor impulse control may have been raised by parents who shared this character trait. In these cases, the children may have inherited the trait biologically, they may have learned the behavior by example, or both. Some theorists believe that the basic physical makeup of impulsive individuals may differ from that of other people. An excess or a deficiency of certain chemicals in the brain may predispose particular people toward acting impulsively. As with so many psychological tendencies, it is likely that a combination of physiological and environmental factors helps shape this character trait. Whatever the cause, however, the result is often disastrous.

Everyone is impulsive at times. But when impulsivity is more than an occasional behavior—when it comes to control a person's entire life—it has left the realm of conduct that is merely improper and may represent a form of mental disorder. In their book *Shadow Syndromes*, Drs. John Ratey and Catherine Johnson of Harvard Medical School state that people who have impulsive character traits tend to "shoot first, ask questions later." The authors add that, for people with poor impulse control, "the reflecting, filtering, censor mechanism all of us require in order to function in the world is impaired." Such individuals seem to be intensely involved in their own activities, here and now, and they have little awareness of the future consequences of their behavior. They are consumed by their immediate predicament, ignoring or angrily rejecting any similarities between past experience and the present situation. People with this problem are often unable to resist the urge to engage in acts that could be harmful to them or to others.

People with poor impulse control live only in the present. Sometimes they are aware that their lives are taking a steady, downhill course, but they are unable to stop their destructive behavior. Although they may manage to slow the downturn, they often feel incapable of turning their lives around. They consider themselves victims, and they may even use their sense of powerlessness as an excuse for living for the moment. In desperation or anger, they pursue fleeting pleasures that always prove to be less satisfying than they had hoped.

WHAT ARE IMPULSE-CONTROL DISORDERS?

Impulsivity is present in a number of mental disorders. In many individuals this characteristic may be severe enough to be considered a problem but not severe enough to be listed under "Impulse-Control

In some cases, a connection exists between an impulse-control disorder and another psychological disturbance. Drug abuse is one of the problems sometimes associated with poor impulse control.

Disorders" in the *DSM-IV*. According to the *DSM-IV*—a manual that describes the symptoms, prevalence, and treatment for each type of mental disorder for which health care providers can collect medical insurance—in order for a particular form of impulsivity to be classified as an impulse disorder, it must meet certain specific requirements.

The *DSM-IV* states, "The essential feature of Impulse-Control Disorders is the failure to resist an impulse . . . that is harmful to the person or others. For most of the disorders in this [category], the individual feels an increasing sense of tension or arousal before committing the act and then experiences pleasure, gratification, or relief at the time of committing the act. Following the act there may or may not be regret, self-reproach, or guilt."

Impulse-control disorders may also be associated with other mental disorders. These include substance (drug or alcohol) abuse, schizophrenia (a psychosis that causes people to have a distorted sense of reality), antisocial personality and conduct disorders (behavior patterns involving the repeated violation of the rights of others or of societal norms), and mood disorders (which involve mood swings that are extreme in intensity and duration). Five specific impulse-control disorders are listed in the *DSM-IV* that may not appear in conjunction with other problems: *pathological* gambling, kleptomania, pyromania, trichotillomania, and intermittent explosive disorder. A sixth category, "Impulse-Control Disorders Not Otherwise Specified," covers unusual impulse problems with features unique to particular individuals.

Whenever we think about mental disorders, we should keep in mind that many—if not most—psychological problems are not distinct types of diseases (such as pneumonia or diabetes) that are the same from person to person. A doctor may be able to determine that a person has a certain disease simply by the presence of a specific virus. However, the definitions given in the *DSM-IV* are merely lists of qualities that, when considered together, paint a certain picture. The details of this picture will vary from person to person, and there is no absolute criterion for determining the presence or absence of any particular mental disorder.

Nevertheless, because many mental problems spring from neurochemical disorders, they are more like physical illnesses than was once recognized. As science has made new advances, researchers have found that the causes of some mental disorders that were once considered to be purely psychological or emotional stem from physiological problems that produce psychological pain. These mental disorders cannot be cured by psychotherapy ("talk" therapy). Upbringing and other environmental factors certainly contribute to some behavioral problems, but scientists are currently researching the biological or genetic predispositions that may make certain people more likely to develop these problems.

CHARACTERISTICS OF IMPULSE-CONTROL DISORDERS

It is clear that, when we talk about mental disorders, the neat classifications that separate one type of disorder from the next are not exactly realistic. The *DSM-IV* may help us classify and study problems, but it is important to remember that problems that afflict different people never manifest themselves in exactly the same way. Studying one case history can give us insights into another person's situation, but each case ultimately must be studied on its own terms.

The classification of disorders suggests more standardization than reality provides. However, we can set forth the characteristics that most people with poor impulse control seem to have in common.

SELF-CENTEREDNESS

People with poor impulse control may reject the social norms and restraints that threaten their impulsivity. Their disappointment with life may prompt them to lash out at family, friends, and society. They may feel justified in hurting others because they consider themselves to be victims. They may believe they have a right to behave as they please because they feel that they have had less than others from the start. They may be intelligent and charming without ever demonstrating any real concern for others. Individuals who experience impulsiveness that is *chronic* (that persists for a very long time) may copy other people's outward style and behaviors but lack the ability to maintain sincere, long-lasting relationships.

People with these disorders may view themselves as the principal actors in a play, with everyone else making up the supporting cast. In extreme cases, they may injure others without showing any evidence of remorse or compassion. Or they may show grief in order to elicit a desired reaction from others.

FAILURE TO LEARN FROM PAST MISTAKES

People with poor impulse control tend to replay their personal problems in whatever setting they find themselves. In other words, in marriage, employment, prison, or health care settings, they repeat the same mistakes. Although the actors may change, the script remains the same. Impulsive behavior is referred to as *maladaptive* because it makes the person's life more difficult. An individual with poor impulse control will not note the error of his or her ways and then correct the behavior in the future. For instance, the pathological gambler doesn't learn that gambling is like making a bad investment—the longer the gambling continues, the surer the odds are that he or she will lose. Instead, the person yields again and again to the impulse to gamble. Poor impulse control then becomes a *compulsion*—the psychological need to repeat a behavior over and over.

CHARACTERISTICS COMMON TO ALL IMPULSE-CONTROL DISORDERS

In order to be diagnosed as having an impulse-control disorder, an individual must demonstrate the following characteristics:

1. failure to resist an impulse or temptation, even if the act would be harmful to the individual or to others;
2. a growing sense of tension or excitement before committing the act; and
3. a sense of pleasure, gratification, or release at the time of committing the act or shortly thereafter.

ORIGINATION IN CHILDHOOD

Impulse-control disorders often begin in childhood. The young person who is impulsive soon fails to see his or her conduct as abnormal. As inappropriate behaviors are repeated again and again, destructive behavior is reinforced. A child who continues to behave in unproductive ways may develop a lack of self-respect. Early recognition and intervention (see the "Treatment" section later in this chapter) can prevent the problem from taking control of a young person's life.

LOW SELF-ESTEEM

People whose destructive behaviors lead to a lack of self-worth may overcompensate for this feeling of emptiness by developing a style of bravado—especially when they are with people they view as different or better. For instance, a young woman may be loud and talkative, or a young man may appear to swagger fearlessly through life. Each person will compensate for the problem in a different way, but the purpose of the compensation will be to cover up the discomfort that the disturbed person feels in the presence of people who don't share a tendency for self-destruction.

Sometimes the slightest insult, intentional or accidental, may trigger a serious confrontation. A fragile sense of self-esteem always hangs in the balance. Nagging self-doubts sometimes inspire the individual to seek self-worth in external achievement without ever resolving the inner problem. Even repeated reassurance of the person's worth does not relieve his or her feelings of worthlessness. In an effort to maintain self-esteem, the individual may take excessive risks to "prove" his or her intelligence, wit, skill, or luck. The person's need to demonstrate that he or she is not a "loser" may cause the individual, for example, to view winning at the crap table, at cards, at the track, or in other gambling arenas as critical.

POOR RELATIONSHIPS

Time and time again, people with impulse-control disorders will experience relationships that fall apart. As a result, these individuals may become aloof, if not aggressive, toward others. They may be unwilling—in fact, unable—to maintain close relationships. As a result, they may use other people without giving of themselves. The feeling that they have been generally shortchanged may make them view taking, rather than giving, as important. Emotional bankruptcy may cause these people to feel that, to even the score on life's balance sheet, they must take from others.

Dr. Howard Wishnie of Harvard Medical School was one of the early researchers of impulse-control disorders. In his book *The Impulsive Personality*, he described two typical cases:

> In spite of numerous involvements with people, Jim states it this way: "It's funny, even with a buddy where I know I should feel something, like sympathy or understanding, you know, I feel nothing. I just kinda go through the motions."
>
> Irv, who was superficially engaging, articulate, and poised, described his avoidance of serious personal involvement this way: "Your worst enemy is having a friend. You're safe if you don't care. Stay cool."

In some cases, such thought and behavior patterns can be traced to childhood experiences in which repeated disappointment led a youngster to give up on relationships and avoid close encounters with others.

Sometimes people who have impulse-control disorders become involved with illegal drugs. Substance abuse merely aggravates the problem, however. It can further erode a person's sense of self-esteem and make maintaining close relationships even more difficult.

The impulsive person may relate to other people in his or her life as though they are unreal or interchangeable. Ultimately, even parents, children, husbands, and wives come to mean little to a person who sees individuals in his or her life as easily replaced. A rapid turnover of friends, companions, and lovers is characteristic of this inability to sustain intimacy.

In *Shadow Syndromes,* Drs. Ratey and Johnson describe the following case of a man with an impulse-control disorder:

> The point of love for him . . . has been to find a woman who could reflect back the image he so desperately needed to see. He tells a story of having lunch not long ago with the woman who was his first wife, and discovering he had no idea who she was, what she wanted in life, her likes and dislikes, the things she found funny— all these details had passed him by. . . . His sole requirement in a lover or mate is that she be his golden mirror.

In *The Impulsive Personality,* Dr. Wishnie quoted one patient's description of the shallowness of feeling that he experienced when his girlfriend ended their relationship: "I was really down when she left. I thought I couldn't go on living. The next day, you wouldn't believe it. I met Rachel and, well, that was it. My life was complete again." For these people, according to Dr. Wishnie, other individuals are as interchangeable as machine parts. Each person serves a specific function, but one is as good as another for providing sexual gratification, companionship, economic support, housecleaning, or any other need. Impulsive individuals will usually switch partners often and minimize the time between the end of one relationship and the beginning of another.

Some people with impulse-control disorders may be capable of injuring another human being—even a close friend or family member—without feeling remorse. For these people, stereotypes frequently replace any real understanding of who other individuals truly are. The role, rather than the person who occupies it, is all that they see. "Mothers aren't supposed to get tired" or "wives should always be supportive" might describe some of the ways that they may view others. One man spoke of women he had dated in the past as "Dina the dancer" or "Arlene the artist," but he rarely mentioned the women's last names and he couldn't remember much about them aside from the roles they filled. When confronted with reality, an impulsive person may become angry or feel disappointed and may even seek revenge.

MANIPULATION OF OTHERS

In the absence of caring relationships, people with impulse-control disorders may become manipulative of friends and family—using others to gratify themselves. They may lie, exaggerate, and twist the truth to get other people to do favors for them. They may even use manipulation as a basic survival skill, priding themselves on their expert "con" jobs.

Behind this behavior is the pervasive insecurity that we discussed previously. A lack of confidence in the ability to accomplish goals on his or her own can cause the person to feel the need to depend on manipulation of others. The individual may believe that, if others knew what he or she really wanted, they would refuse to help. Therefore, trickery and deception become a matter of course.

ACTION VERSUS FEELING

Frequently, people with these disorders act out as a way to avoid facing negative emotions such as sadness, shame, or anger. They resort to gambling, lighting fires, or other such activities that provide enough outer stress to distract them from their inner conflicts. Usually, the impulsive activities only cause more difficulties, creating financial, interpersonal, and legal problems that generate even more stress. Consequently, the "solution" is worse than the original problem the person sought to evade. For example, the gambler may write bad checks to cover debts, lie to family members about his or her whereabouts, steal money to continue gambling, or face arrest for breaking the law. The person's life becomes a self-destructive cycle. Virtually everyone, including the individual him- or herself, focuses on the bad behavior rather than on the problems that are causing it.

INABILITY TO PLAN

People with poor impulse control often have an aversion to any type of planning. They may feel trapped even by their own plans, preferring to remain "spontaneous" or to act erratically rather than stick to a schedule.

As with all of the characteristics of impulse-control disorders, the problem is usually one of degree. Many people who function normally may have difficulty making plans. However, when a problem begins to interfere with a person's ability to carry out the requirements of everyday life, it is more than a minor difficulty—it may indicate a mental disorder.

One impulsive man viewed planning for vacations, for meetings, or for other events as terribly threatening. Even though holidays represented a break from his ordinary routine, the need to choose specific dates and make plane reservations ahead of time generated enormous anxiety. He frequently ended up purchasing tickets at the last minute when the cost was prohibitively high. When he used a travel agent, the man felt compelled to change plans continuously. He could not bring himself to follow a single itinerary. When unforeseen circumstances interfered with his scheduled vacation time, he was incapable of informing others that he would be unavailable on the dates in question. Instead, he constantly changed flight arrangements until finally no travel agent would work with him. His irrational fear of "being trapped" by plans—even his own—kept him from making a schedule and sticking to it.

This impulsive man—like many impulsive individuals—habitually arrived at appointments late. Punctuality requires the ability to think ahead in order to leave enough time to reach a given destination at a given hour. This individual felt that the need to take time into consideration threatened his freedom. The people who might be inconvenienced by his tardiness never entered his mind. We probably all know someone who demonstrates this quality to some extent. But again, as the *DSM-IV* states, a mental disorder may be diagnosed only when there is an "impairment in one or more important areas of functioning," caused by "a behavioral, psychological, or biological dysfunction."

INABILITY TO DELAY GRATIFICATION

The inability to delay gratification—which is a corollary of the inability to plan ahead—is at the root of impulsiveness. The impulsive person feels unable to wait for whatever it is that he or she wants and does not learn from past mistakes in this regard. The desire for immediate gratification is an expression of the individual's underlying sense of neediness. People with poor impulse control are typically impatient, intolerant of delays caused by other people's legitimate needs, and self-centered. They often dominate others, expecting them to carry out their wishes.

These individuals may also have difficulty handling discomfort or pain. They usually demand immediate relief from stress or anxiety. They do not believe that the future will bring relief, so they require help immediately. Infants experience the world in this manner, but their ability to control impulses typically develops with maturity. Parents control children's impulses at first, and youngsters internalize the parents' role later. The person with an impulse-control disorder has been unable to learn this life lesson.

SENSE OF ENTITLEMENT

The impulsive person often adopts a superior manner, insisting that he or she is different from others and deserves special treatment. In some cases, this may be the individual's way of compensating for feelings of inferiority. The person may believe that a different set of rules applies to him or her than to the rest of the world. Obviously, the impulsive individual's needs and impulses cannot be gratified at the expense of the needs and impulses of others if everyone is given the same consideration. Consequently, the impulsive person often cannot admit that others have the same rights that he or she has. The individual may justify this attitude by dwelling on his or her perceived deprivation as a child. The kleptomaniac, for instance, may steal to make up for needs—such as love—that he or she believes were not fulfilled during childhood. The impulsive person may feel entitled to be late, to have more income (which he or she may expect that the fates will provide through "luck" at the track or other gambling establishments), to destroy property, or—in general—to gratify him- or herself immediately.

People with impulse-control disorders may feel uncomfortable with limits. They may react negatively to being told "no." They may fail to set limits for themselves. Eventually, family members, friends, the community, or the law may step in to stop them from engaging in destructive behaviors.

REBELLIOUSNESS

A person with poor impulse control may see him- or herself in opposition to family members who have wronged him or her in some way. The individual may see all choices in terms of either rebellion against authority or conformity to it. School authorities, government, and other parental surrogates such as husbands, wives, therapists, police, and employers replace parental authority figures. Impulsive people may perceive their sense of identity as threatened whenever they obey these authorities, who set limits and say "no," and they may feel a sense of freedom when they follow their own impulses instead. In fact, such contrariness is not a free expression of identity, however, because every act is determined by an outside force that the rebel must reject. Being the

Rebelling against authority, as these teenagers have done by adopting an unconventional appearance, is often a normal aspect of adolescence. In some instances, however, rebellion is a symptom of more serious problems.

disobedient "bad boy" or "bad girl" provides a sense of self, but it is a negative sense of self. What can begin as juvenile delinquency can give way to more severe problems as the person grows older.

TREATMENT

Recovery from any mental disorder takes time. Just as a problem may develop or worsen over a period of years, improvement can be gradual and uneven. However, even if complete recovery does not occur, marked progress is possible and important. Achieving mental health can be a lifelong process. Although we tend to think of sickness or health as absolute categories, when it comes to mental health, we encounter a wide range of behaviors. Because all of us are impulsive once in a while, we cannot expect that recovery will mean the complete disappearance of this symptom.

A critical step with impulse-control disorders is a person's recognition of the problem and desire to change his or her behavior. People suffer from different degrees of impulse-control disorders, and over time some individuals may learn to mask the disorder or come to view it as part of their identity. Therapy can be effective only if the sufferer admits that there is a problem.

Sometimes impulse-control disorders go unchecked for years or even decades—until, for instance, a man who gambles compulsively has lost so much money that his distraught family finally brings him in for therapy. Or a woman who suffers from kleptomania may engage in denial until she is caught shoplifting or stealing expensive items. Then the criminal justice system may force her to confront the problem or seek professional help. Similarly, a pyromaniac who can't keep from lighting fires may eventually end up in prison or in a psychiatric hospital, where he or she can begin to receive treatment for an extremely dangerous ailment. The sooner that recognition and intervention take place, the sooner recovery can begin.

Because a single condition can manifest itself in different ways in different people, a treatment that may help one individual may prove ineffective for another. In many cases, however—especially when a patient recognizes his or her problem and seeks to change the behavior associated with it—individual and family counseling can alleviate or even eliminate the symptoms connected with poor impulse control.

Games of chance have been in use since as far back as biblical times. Today gambling exists in many forms—from cockfights to the stock market—in virtually every culture.

2

PATHOLOGICAL GAMBLING

Tim doesn't think he has a problem. He just likes to have a good time betting on the horses at the racetrack. There's nothing wrong with that, he tells himself. His mother is dying of cancer, and Tim needs somewhere he can go to escape from the anxiety and depression he feels when he thinks about his mother. Whenever he places a bet, he gets a "high" that drives the worries right out of his head.

Lately, Tim has had a string of bad luck, but he's not worried about that. He knows that any day now the right horse will come along and he'll win big. Deep inside him, he has this feeling that "lady luck" understands that he deserves a windfall after all he's been through.

That same feeling drives Tim to place bigger bets against greater odds. As a result, he's run a little short of cash lately. He may need to persuade a friend to lend him a few hundred dollars, just until his big win, or he may decide to borrow some funds from his company's petty cash box. Either way, he can hardly wait until his next visit to the races. In fact, he finds that, even when he's at his mother's bedside, he can think of nothing but the next bet he'll place.

Tim doesn't realize it, but he has a serious problem. His gambling is no longer recreational. Somewhere along the way, it became pathological. In fact, Tim's behavior meets all of the *DSM-IV* criteria for pathological gambling.

GAMBLING AS A CULTURAL PHENOMENON

In the United States, cultural attitudes toward gambling vary greatly. Some people consider gambling, at best, a sign of stupidity—choosing to risk money when the odds are stacked against them—and, at worst, a sin. Others are attracted to gambling because they see it as an opportunity to "get rich quick"— to beat the system by making money without working for a living. Still others have a neutral view of gambling, considering it to be merely a game, like bowling, in which money is spent to pass time in the company of friends. Events on which people place wagers can take different forms, ranging from cockfights—in which two roosters are pitted against each other in a fight to the death—to the game of jai alai and from horse races to the stock market. In the United States, gambling has become big business, even helping to balance state budgets through government-sponsored lotteries.

George Bernard Shaw said that "gambling promises for the poor what property does for the rich: Something for nothing." Behind this flip remark lies an understanding that gambling questions a social order built on the notion that people get what they deserve as the fruits of their labor. Gambling offers a small minority the hope of unearned wealth. On a practical level, of course, many people approve of lotteries. Thomas Jefferson saw the lottery as "a wonderful thing: It lays taxation only on the willing."

But Jefferson was not entirely correct. Gambling—like drinking alcohol and smoking cigarettes—does not represent free choice for those who are addicted. With impulse-control disorders, the will to decide how the person wants to act is no longer within his or her power.

HISTORICAL ORIGINS OF GAMBLING

RELIGIOUS PRACTICES

The word *lot* and its Teutonic root *bleut* go back to the term for *pebble*, because a pebble was cast to decide disputes and divide property. Games of chance, such as throwing dice, were originally religious rituals used to determine God's will. In the Bible, for example, drawing lots was used in circumstances as diverse as electing a king (1 Samuel 10:20–21), identifying those guilty of sacrilege (Joshua 7:10–26), selecting a date to engage in future actions (Esther 3:7, 9:24), and choosing a scapegoat for sins committed (Leviticus 16:8–10). During a storm, sailors drew lots to determine whom they should sacrifice. When the lot fell to Jonah, he was cast into the sea (Jonah 1:7). Similar practices are found among other peoples, in Greek mythology, in pre-Islamic Arabia, among Muslims, and in different countries around the world. Excavators found loaded dice in the ruins of Pompeii, and marked playing cards (used for cheating) date back to the 14th century. As late as the 16th century, borough officers in England were occasionally chosen by lot.

Religious practices frequently reflect deep-seated psychological notions. The ancient practice of human and animal sacrifice gave way to the sacrifice of produce and money to good causes or to the gods. Even people who don't believe in God theologically may feel on some level that, if they fail to pay for their good fortune, they'll lose their undeserved rewards. A distinguished college professor once noted that, whenever he received a job promotion or other honor, he would misplace his expensive camera equipment (much of which was never found). In psychological counseling, the professor came to realize that, unconsciously, losing his beloved cameras was his way of appeasing the fates. Similarly, some people gamble not because they fool themselves into believing that they might win but because they have a subconscious need to lose (sacrifice) money as a token of thanks for life's undeserved gifts or as a plea for forgiveness for shameful actions. Gambling is a more complex psychological activity than it appears to be at first glance.

BIG BUSINESS

The governments in both Great Britain and the United States restricted gambling throughout much of the 19th and 20th centuries. Although it may seem to some individuals that people should be allowed to throw their money around as they wish, society has viewed gambling—like taking drugs—as particularly dangerous for some individuals, if not for the greater community. Widespread efforts to control gambling resulted. With the exception of Nevada, which permitted gambling establishments to prosper, most states outlawed betting—whether on card games, horse races, sports events, or slot machines. In the second half of the 20th century, however, 22 American states legalized casino gambling, and most states came to accept some form of legal gambling. Potential revenues for governments, churches, businesses, and other interests proved too tempting.

Controlled betting industries began to grow as the U.S. government made exceptions. In the United States alone, commercial gambling was generating gross revenues of $45 billion by 1995. Gambling observers estimate that the amount of money wagered illegally is four times the amount wagered legally. Research conducted by the National Council on Compulsive Gambling indicates that 80 percent of Americans participate in some form of gambling behavior (though only 3 to 5 percent gamble beyond the point where they'd like to stop). Predictions put annual gambling revenues by the year 2000 at about $400 per capita, or in excess of $100 billion each year (upward of 2 percent of Americans' annual income).

As various state governments have legalized casino gambling in the last half-century, controlled betting industries have boomed. Annual gambling revenues in the United States are now estimated at $100 billion.

On some Native American reservations, residents have been able to establish legal gambling operations despite state laws that prohibit such establishments. This is because Native American lands are, in some respects, considered to be sovereign nations whose residents can create their own laws to a certain degree. In southeastern Connecticut, for example, some 250 Native Americans on the Mashantucket Pequot reservation were able to set up a lucrative casino in spite of Connecticut statutes that outlaw gambling.

The Pequot tribe installed acres of slot machines; blackjack, poker, and crap tables; tellers to take bets on nearly every horse track in the land; television monitors to display results from Chicago, New Jersey, Florida, and Maryland; and bingo halls that charged as much as $350 for admission. The operation has brought the Pequot people great wealth.

Currently, sports wagers on the Internet and offshore betting represent a technological equivalent to the Native American exception from gambling regulations. The federal government is seeking to control gambling on the Internet and through companies that either operate in places such as Aruba to take long-distance bets from Americans or are actually based in the United States but pretend to be located in foreign countries.

In recent years, Native Americans living on reservations have established a number of legal gambling operations. This successful casino in Albuquerque, New Mexico, for example, shares land with the reservation's grazing cattle.

Computerized slot and jackpot machines, increased access to instant credit through credit cards, and growing numbers of stock and commodities options have greatly expanded the quantity and variety of gambling opportunities that are available today and that will be available in the near future. In addition, advances in communication and transportation—by air, sea, and land—make gambling establishments in Monte Carlo, Atlantic City, Las Vegas, and the Caribbean Islands; on cruise ships; and elsewhere more accessible to greater numbers of people.

PATHOLOGICAL GAMBLING

An activity that generates as much capital as gambling does, even when regulated, is obviously not financed by a small group of people with mental disorders. The numbers make it clear that gambling has enough popular appeal for it to be classified as "normal." In any population, however, a certain percentage of people will become so obsessed with gambling that it will consume both their lives and their resources. *The Gambler*, written by Russian novelist Fyodor Dostoyevsky in 1866, captures the thought pattern of a pathological gambler as the narrator describes his own gambling: "Perhaps passing through so many sensations, my soul was not more satisfied, but only irritated by them, and craved still more sensations—and stronger ones till utterly exhausted.... I really was suddenly overcome by terrible craving for risk."

Money, the fuel on which gambling runs, has symbolic meaning as well as objective worth. Money may represent virility for a man whose injury, old age, retirement, or disability has stripped him of the ability to provide for his family after a lifetime of working. In desperation, people who have lost other means of earning money can misinterpret gambling as a form of work. The transition from recreational gambling to compulsive gambling can occur gradually or develop in response to some source of stress, such as a life-threatening illness or job loss.

The *DSM-IV* specifies that, for problem gambling to be classified as pathological gambling, it must be "persistent and recurrent," disrupting a person's work and/or family life. The individual must be preoccupied with gambling and may be consumed with reliving past gambling experiences or with planning for, or coming up with ways to finance, future gambling ventures. Most pathological gamblers describe themselves as seeking "action"—which produces an aroused, euphoric state—even more than money. Increasingly larger bets or greater risks may become necessary to produce the desired level of excitement.

For gambling to be considered pathological, rather than recreational or professional, it must be persistent, recurrent, and disruptive to the individual's life. In the movie Rounders, *Matt Damon— shown here at a poker table— risks his law school career and his relationship with his girlfriend when he becomes caught up in the gambling circuit.*

Gambling may represent a way for the person to escape feelings of helplessness, guilt, anxiety, or depression. As such, attempts to curtail gambling can make the individual feel nervous, restless, or irritable. To compensate, the gambler may come to take greater and more irrational risks, abandoning a safer betting strategy in order to "chase" losses.

Pathological gambling leads to other problems as well. The compulsive gambler frequently lies to family members, counselors, and friends to conceal the extent of his or her gambling. In *Behind the 8-Ball*, Dr. Linda Berman and Dr. Mary-Ellen Siegel describe an elderly man who was unpleasantly surprised by the secret gambling losses of his wife, Hattie. Hattie had always managed the family finances, and her husband had never thought to question her on money matters. When he began to suggest that the time had come to look for a place to retire, however, Hattie just kept stalling and making excuses not to go with him. One day, though, Hattie's husband found what he thought would be the perfect place for them. He asked Hattie to show him the bank accounts so he could calculate exactly how much they could afford. To his dismay, he discovered that they had no savings at all. Hattie's "little" day trips to Atlantic City had totally wiped out their retirement fund.

When sources of funding become strained, the person who gambles pathologically may resort to unlawful practices, such as forgery, fraud, theft, or embezzlement to acquire money. Berman and Siegel point out that most crimes committed by gamblers are nonviolent: "They commit forgery, siphon money from business to personal accounts, or 'con' the public with financial get-rich-quick schemes. Many turn to insurance fraud by creating or staging accidents, committing arson, or faking business, home, or personal burglaries." As a result, these individuals jeopardize significant relationships, jobs, or educational opportunities in order to keep gambling.

Ultimately, after squandering all available resources, pathological gamblers turn to family and friends to bail them out. Even when the compulsive gambler requests economic help, however, he or she usually denies having a problem and assumes little responsibility for the behavior, insisting that it's just a run of bad luck. Berman and Siegel point out that, when circumstances finally make denial of the problem completely unbelievable, the gambler will typically convince him- or herself that all losses will be "magically restored."

OTHER FEATURES OF PATHOLOGICAL GAMBLING

Denial is one form of distorted thinking exhibited by pathological gamblers. Others include overconfidence and delusions of grandeur. Despite repeated losses, the gambler may feel convinced that he or she can't lose. Rather than face the real source of his or her troubles, the gambler may refer to a desperate financial situation as "a temporary cash-flow problem." Another example of the "magical thinking" that Berman and Siegel discuss is the development of superstitions. Perennial gamblers may look for betting signs or omens in the most unlikely places. Typically, compulsive gamblers consider money both the cause of and the solution to all their problems.

Pathological gamblers are often highly competitive people who are generally energetic, restless, and easily bored. Some are overly concerned with approval and are generous to the point of extravagance. Excess, rather than moderation, is a common character trait. When they are not gambling, they are typically either workaholics or "binge" workers, who wait until they are facing deadlines and then push themselves (and others) mercilessly. They may be prone to the development of medical conditions associated with stress, such as hypertension, peptic ulcers, or migraine headaches. Other disorders that have been found among compulsive gamblers include mood disorders, substance abuse or dependence, *narcissism* (a selfish, egocentric love of oneself), antisocial behavior, and *attention-deficit disorder* (ADD) and *hyperactivity.* (ADD is a set of learning and behavior problems that interfere with a person's ability to pay attention. When it is accompanied by hyperactivity—a condition in which individuals are abnormally active—it is known as attention-deficit/hyperactivity disorder, or ADHD.)

According to the *DSM-IV,* pathological gamblers make up 2 to 3 percent of the adult population. The illness is far more common among men than among women—about two-thirds of pathological gamblers are male. Females are underrepresented in treatment programs, however: women make up only about 2 to 4 percent of the membership of Gamblers Anonymous (see the "Treatment" section in this chapter for more information about this organization). One of the many reasons for this gender difference may be that women hesitate to seek treatment because traditionally in our society gambling has been considered more acceptable for men than for women. It is more common for women than for men with this disorder to gamble as an escape from depression.

Pathological gambling typically begins in adolescence for boys and later in life for girls. As with alcohol dependence, offspring of families where gambling is a problem have an increased chance of developing the disorder. Although a few individuals seem to get "hooked" with their very first bet, the process is more insidious for most gamblers—that is, the problem tends to develop gradually. The gambling can be regular or episodic, but the disorder is usually chronic. Periods of stress or depression may increase the motivation for and the frequency of gambling.

PATHOLOGICAL VERSUS PROFESSIONAL OR SOCIAL GAMBLING

Pathological gambling should be distinguished from professional gambling or social gambling. Social gambling normally takes place among friends or acquaintances, in a limited amount of time with predetermined risks. Professional gambling is disciplined rather than compulsive and is usually conducted with strangers. For example, people who participate in a friendly game of weekly poker, with a pot of $10, would not be considered pathological gamblers. Similarly, in most cases, although the owners of gambling establishments bet house money against the money of their patrons on a daily basis, they gamble professionally rather than compulsively or pathologically. The *DSM-IV* criteria for pathological gambling are similar to those for abuse disorders. Pathological gamblers are compulsive risk takers who lack limits when it comes to betting. For them, gambling is an *addiction*—a compulsive need for a substance or activity that is known to be harmful.

Compulsive gambling is sometimes likened to addictive behavior. Weekly horse track betting, for example, is merely a social activity for some. For others, however, it can lead to an uncontrollable need for the stimulation it provides.

PATHOLOGICAL GAMBLING AS AN ADDICTION OR MANIA

Many clinicians consider excessive gambling a type of addictive behavior. In the absence of chemical substances, of course, the word *addiction* is something of a metaphor for compulsive activity. Nevertheless, just as research into alcoholism that runs in families has uncovered a biological, hereditary predisposition to alcoholism or drug addiction in some people, a predilection toward gambling may have physical as well as psychological sources. It is possible that a person's craving for the stimulation of gambling, for example, may stem from his or her particular biochemical or genetic makeup.

Pathological gambling can be confused with a mood disorder that sometimes accompanies compulsive gambling—*bipolar disorder*, a condition in which *mania* (an excited state in which a person feels agitated or restless) alternates with a depressed state. Although pathological gamblers may behave as though they are manic while winning, if mania disappears when the person leaves the gambling environment, a diagnosis of bipolar disorder is clearly inappropriate. Research in R. A. McCormick and J. I. Taber's *Handbook on Pathologic Gambling* indicates that a high percentage of gamblers experience major depression when they are not gambling. Gambling may act for these people in the same way as an *antidepressant* (a medication used to relieve or prevent feelings of depression). The manic and depressive cycles of a person with bipolar disorder parallel the high-energy euphoria of the winning gambler and the desperate lows of the losing gambler.

TREATMENT

In 1939, a self-support organization called Alcoholics Anonymous (AA) was formed to help people who were addicted to alcohol. The organization developed a 12-step treatment program, supplemented by self-revelation and support groups, that has proved successful over the years. Although substance abuse or physiological intoxication is not a feature of pathological gambling, the founders of Gamblers Anonymous (GA), Gam-Anon (for families and spouses), and Gam-Ateen (for adolescent children of people with a gambling disorder) use the same basic 12-step model to treat compulsive gambling.

Gamblers Anonymous and its sister organizations are important resources for people who gamble pathologically. It is a fellowship that encourages abstinence as well as emotional and spiritual growth (although it is not affiliated with any religion). The underlying concept

THE PHILOSOPHY OF TREATMENT

Most treatment programs for gamblers share a common philosophy represented by the acronym THERAPIES:

T = Team approach is taken by a well-qualified, multidisciplinary staff.

H = "Here-and-now" focus on the patient's repertoire and problems is encouraged.

E = Educational modules on compulsive gambling and other addictive disorders are taught.

R = Restitution of all gambling-related debts and review of financial problems are made.

A = Abstinence from all gambling activities is required.

P = Physical problems are treated, and physical fitness is stressed.

I = Individual, group, marital, and family therapies are pursued.

E = Evaluation and management of character flaws and of maladaptive coping skills are performed.

S = Self-support groups such as Gamblers Anonymous (GA) are integrated into the program. Aftercare, following discharge, helps prevent relapse. Groups such as GA provide ongoing support.

is that people with similar problems can help each other. The only necessary requirement for participating in GA is the desire to quit gambling.

In addition to Gamblers Anonymous, treatment options include inpatient and outpatient programs, residential care, halfway houses, contract therapy, *behavior modification* (a form of therapy that uses reinforcement techniques to teach desirable behaviors and eliminate undesirable behaviors), individual and group therapy, and traditional psychoanalysis. Whatever therapy is used, however, recovery is difficult and relapses are common.

FAMILIES OF PATHOLOGICAL GAMBLERS

Profiles of the spouses of compulsive gamblers sometimes reveal partners with passive-dependent personalities who feel trapped in their

Group therapy and self-help groups have become important aspects of treatment programs for pathological gamblers. In this session, for instance, patients offer one another support by sharing their own successes and failures in the battle against compulsive gambling.

marriages. Although the wife of a pathological gambler may be impressed by her husband's outgoing manner, she will often practice denial about her husband's gambling. She may lack self-esteem or assertiveness, or she may function as an *enabler* for her husband's disorder. (An enabler is a person who makes it easier for another individual's undesirable behavior to continue—by making excuses for it, helping to hide it, and the like.) To treat what is sometimes termed *codependency*—a condition in which someone is controlled or manipulated by an addicted individual—the entire family may receive counseling. Family therapists then face the task of preventing overgeneralization that might relieve the gambler of responsibility for his actions by spreading the guilt. When families of pathological gamblers have suffered physical or psychological abuse at the hands of the gambler, counseling for family members is certainly in order. But the responsibility for pathological gambling and the need for change rest primarily with the compulsive gambler and not with his or her victims.

It is not uncommon for the children of a man who gambles compulsively to be swept into an alliance with their mother to pressure their father to stop betting and start fulfilling his obligations to the family. In these cases, youngsters may take on parental roles toward the gambling parent. These children may need help coping with not only their feelings of fear, frustration, anger, resentment, guilt, depression, anxiety, or confusion but also the financial insecurity created by the gambler. For these youngsters, the sense of neglect, abandonment, pain, and deceit experienced by their mothers when their fathers relinquish their duties as parents and breadwinners can be extremely upsetting. A wedge can develop between the children and the gambling parent who is constantly breaking promises. Children may try to shame or scold the parent into more appropriate behavior.

Conversely, an underlying fear of abandonment can make the children of gamblers seek approval from the gambling parent or deny his or her negative actions. Like the offspring of all types of addicts, these youngsters are typically saddled with a long history of disappointment. Some develop defenses against the loss and the psychic pain. Some become extremely involved in school clubs, sports, and other activities in an attempt to escape a *dysfunctional* (unhealthy) home life. Others may fail to make close friends as they try to hide or deny a gambling problem. Still others may use numerous superficial relationships to compensate for a difficult home life.

As children of a father who gambles compulsively grow older, some try to protect their mother, even though they feel anxious about financial insecurities they are powerless to correct. Children often think they must take sides in family disputes, particularly when marital separation or divorce occurs. Clearly, innocent family members, in addition to the compulsive gambler, can profit from counseling. It is important for family members to understand that they are not responsible for the gambler's behavior and that they should not blame themselves for being unable to stop it.

Sometimes family members may even resist the gambler's recovery. These are some of the reasons:

- Recovery may change the family structure, rearranging the roles assigned to each member.

- Recovery may change the family rules (for instance, how confrontations, "secrets," money, and leisure time are handled).
- Recovery may force family members to look at how they have been managing their own emotional needs. (They may have come to depend on being needed, for instance, or they may have gotten attention for being victims.)

But as the gambler begins to recover, therapy can help family members express resentment and guilt about the past and establish new ways of relating to each other. If relapse is prevented, a new sense of trust among family members can be established.

Unfortunately, relapses are fairly common. Financial crises may give the pathological gambler an excuse to return to gambling. Or the compulsive gambler may provoke rejection from family members in order to provide an excuse to resume the negative behavior. Recognition of such maneuvers can help head them off, however. Good therapy reinforces family structure, establishes new covenants among family members, explores appropriate roles and boundaries, and preserves the family system while the gambler recovers.

Although teenage shoplifting can be a serious problem, it does not always indicate kleptomania. For a diagnosis of kleptomania to apply, the need to steal—rather than the need or desire for a specific item—must be the driving force.

3

KLEPTOMANIA—
THE COMPULSIVE NEED
TO STEAL

L iz Smith has a secret. She gets good grades in high school, and she is popular with her friends, but Liz does something she hopes none of her friends or her teachers will ever find out about. Once or twice a week, Liz goes to the drugstore and steals something.

Liz steals only little things—makeup, hand lotion, cough drops. She doesn't know why she takes them. She has enough money to pay for them, and sometimes she doesn't even use what she takes. All Liz knows is that every few days she starts to feel more and more tense, and all she can think about is stealing something. Once she goes to the store and slips something into her purse or inside her sweater, she feels a rush of excitement. Some of her friends once persuaded her to try some illegal drugs, but Liz thinks stealing gives her a far better "high."

Liz's mother and stepfather have a two-year-old daughter. All their attention is lavished on Liz's little sister, and they barely seem to notice what a good student Liz is. Sometimes Liz feels that her mother and stepfather keep her around only to help baby-sit. It has occurred to Liz that maybe she steals to make up for the lack of attention from her parents. But even though she understands this, she can't stop stealing.

Liz is terrified that one day she'll get caught. Then she knows she'll be in really big trouble. She feels so guilty and ashamed—but she still keeps stealing.

Liz's problem has a name: kleptomania. The disorder involves a repeated failure to resist the impulse to steal, even when the sufferer does not need the items for personal use or for their monetary value. Kleptomania differs from occasional shoplifting or the desperate act of a person who steals out of need—kleptomania involves the *desire* to steal more than the *need* for what is taken. A person with kleptomania feels pleasure, gratification, and relief while stealing. However, these feelings may compensate for some underlying sense

Contrary to the message in the sign in this store window, the average person could not distinguish an individual with kleptomania from anyone else. For people who suffer from kleptomania, shoplifting is generally a spur-of-the-moment behavior. They rarely plan the act in advance, and they typically feel guilty after having committed it.

of neediness. Typically, the objects stolen are of little value to the individual, who could well afford to pay for them. Often, after stealing the items, the person gives them away, discards them, hoards them, or secretly returns them.

For the person with kleptomania, stealing is not an expression of anger, vengeance, or some political motive. Neither is it part of a delusional or hallucinogenic experience. In other words, a rioter who breaks into and steals from a store, a political terrorist who takes government property, or a man who believes he is king and therefore entitled to any and all of the nation's goods could not be considered a kleptomaniac.

Although people who suffer from kleptomania are aware that they risk arrest, they take that chance because they can't resist the impulse to steal. They don't usually plan a theft in advance, and they rarely commit the crime with the assistance of others. They realize that stealing is wrong and typically feel guilty about their actions. Psychologists refer to people with this problem as *ego-dystonic*, which indicates that they can't stop themselves from stealing even though they know it's wrong. Individuals with this disorder often worry about getting caught, and the shame that their behavior causes them can lead to depression. Mood disorders, eating disorders, and anxiety disorders are frequently associated with kleptomania. And getting caught in the act can cause legal, family, and employment problems.

Unlike ordinary stealing, kleptomania is quite rare. According to the *DSM-IV*, only about 5 percent of shoplifters are kleptomaniacs. In contrast to compulsive gambling, which is more common among men, this impulse-control disorder usually afflicts women. Even in cases involving repeated apprehension and conviction, the disorder can persist for years. The *DSM-IV* identifies three different courses for the disease:

1. *sporadic stealing*, in which the person engages in brief periods of theft and long periods of remission,

2. *episodic stealing*, in which protracted periods of stealing alternate with intervals when no thefts take place, and

3. *chronic stealing*, in which the individual steals constantly.

Kleptomania is a mental disorder, not a moral failing. Some percentage of regular car thieves and burglars don't recognize what they are doing as wrong. Similarly, some adolescents may shoplift on a dare, to see if they can get away with committing a crime, or to obtain desired items that they can't afford. These are not acts that indicate kleptomania. Kleptomania is not an act of rebellion, a rite of passage, or an antisocial gesture. People with kleptomania generally feel terrible about what they are doing and frequently don't understand their own behavior.

A person with this disorder will typically sense a growing tension immediately before stealing. Once the theft has been completed, however, a flood of relief washes over the individual. The person has no delusions about his or her actions. For example, the individual doesn't believe that he or she is the owner of the store or a Robin Hood–like outlaw who is robbing the rich to give to the poor. As with those who are

A FAMOUS KLEPTOMANIAC

Hedy Lamarr was born in 1913 to a wealthy Austrian family. By the 1930s, she had established a successful movie career in Europe. But when her husband became a Nazi sympathizer, she fled both her marriage and her country. By the late 1930s, Hedy's acting career was flourishing in the United States, but she seemed to sabotage her own success by turning down lead roles in major films. She was difficult to work with—temperamental and moody. And Hedy Lamarr had another problem—she couldn't stop stealing.

Hedy Lamarr's problem was no secret. Her beautiful face was famous, and fans were eager to hear any gossip that concerned her. Hedy handled her disorder in a matter-of-fact way: She simply hired a private secretary to accompany her whenever she went to a store. Hedy would take what she pleased, and, before they left the store, the secretary would quietly pay for whatever items her employer had pilfered.

Hedy Lamarr's personal problems eventually led to financial problems, however, and her movie career failed. But Hedy was not just a beautiful movie star. She also had a brilliant scientific mind, and she helped to invent the technology that we use today in cell phones, pagers, garage door openers, cordless telephones, and defense satellites.

Despite all her talents, though, Hedy continued to suffer from kleptomania. In 1966 she was arrested for shoplifting. Many years later, she was apprehended for stealing makeup and a laxative from a drugstore, but the store opted to drop the charges because of negative publicity.

addicted to drugs or alcohol, people who suffer from kleptomania simply succumb to an overwhelming urge that they cannot resist.

Because kleptomania is a relatively rare disorder, experts have not researched it as thoroughly as they have researched some other disorders. However, studies have produced some data that give a clearer picture of this illness. *The American Psychiatric Press* [APP] *Textbook of Psychiatry* cites the following data: In a 1991 article in the *American*

The Austrian-born film star Hedy Lamarr, shown here at the height of her career, suffered from kleptomania throughout her life. Before her death in January 2000, she was arrested twice for shoplifting.

Journal of Psychiatry, researcher M. J. Goldman concluded that the "typical" person with kleptomania is a 35-year-old woman who began to steal when she was 20 years old. He also estimated that kleptomania occurs in about 6 out of every 1,000 persons. According to a study by S. L. McElroy and colleagues published in 1991 (also cited in the APP textbook), people who have this disorder steal an average of 27 times a month, though there are those who will steal as often as 120 times a

Although kleptomania usually begins in young adulthood, it can persist into the later years. Researchers estimate that the disorder generally lasts between 3 and 38 years.

month. The researchers also estimated that the disorder lasts an average of 16 years, though its duration may be as short as 3 years or as long as 38 years.

TREATMENT

Because kleptomania is relatively uncommon, researchers have not yet come to a consensus on the most effective treatment for the disorder. The shame associated with this condition further complicates the problem. Unless the person is caught in the act of stealing by law enforcement or store security personnel, he or she is apt to keep the thefts a secret, even from counselors or therapists.

According to the book *Impulsivity and Compulsivity*, edited by John M. Oldham, Eric Hollander, and Andrew E. Skodol, psychotherapy alone is not usually an effective treatment for kleptomania. In other words, even if environmental factors have caused the kleptomania, simply answering the question "Why?" does little good. The text indicates that behavior modification techniques are more effective in treating the disorder. *The American Psychiatric Press Textbook of Psychiatry* cites similar reports of success using various behavior modification treatments. The APP textbook also reports that McElroy and colleagues have cited several reports of successful treatment with electrotherapy (in which a controlled burst of electricity is delivered to the patient's brain). And it cites a research study by Dr. A. Burstein that involves a patient diagnosed with biochemical imbalances that caused compulsive stealing. The kleptomania ceased after the patient received medication that countered the imbalances.

The most recent research indicates that many impulse-control disorders are caused by a lack of the chemical *serotonin* (which allows messages to be passed from nerve to nerve) in the brain. In several cases described by E. Lepkifer and associates in a 1999 article in the journal *Clinical Neuropharmacology*, patients were treated with a medication that corrected this deficiency, and the compulsive stealing completely disappeared. When the medication was interrupted, the kleptomania reappeared.

The book *Impulsivity and Compulsivity* suggests that the most effective treatment of kleptomania usually involves a combination of therapies, including medication, psychotherapy, and behavior modification. Cleptomaniacs and Shoplifters Anonymous (CASA) is a self-help group

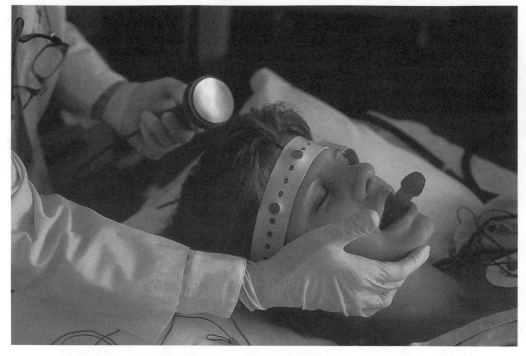

Electrotherapy—also called shock therapy—has been used with some success to treat individuals with kleptomania. This treatment, shown here, uses electric current to induce controlled seizures that can alleviate the symptoms of the disorder.

that can help recovering individuals prevent relapses. CASA models some of its principles after those of Alcoholics Anonymous and Gamblers Anonymous.

CASE HISTORIES

ANNE

Anne is a 36-year-old mother who was employed full time when she entered treatment for kleptomania. She began exhibiting daily signs of kleptomania at the age of 14 or 15. Anne says that she shoplifted, on average, four times a day. She described a near constant urge to steal that she found impossible to control. She also suffered from the rapid mood and energy swings that characterize bipolar disorder. Anne was hospitalized for both severe depression and kleptomania.

Upon discharge from the hospital, Anne was given a medication that aggravated, rather than relieved, her symptoms. She began stealing seven to eight times a day, nearly twice her previous rate. The psychiatrists handling the case hypothesized that her kleptomania might be related to bipolar disorder. Perhaps both disorders would respond to a mood stabilizer. To test this theory, the doctors gave Anne another drug designed to help even out her emotions biochemically. Within a month, Anne began to improve, and when the dosage was increased, she stopped stealing for the first time in her life. After eight months of treatment, Anne reports mild but manageable mood swings, and she no longer feels the impulse to steal. In fact, she has not had a single recurrence of kleptomania.

DEBBIE

Debbie, a 24-year-old woman who lived with her parents, sought treatment for depression after her boyfriend broke up with her. In therapy, she revealed that from time to time she would steal small items from the grocery store. She usually threw away the stolen goods once she got home.

Debbie's father was a domineering man. Her mother was meek and subservient, never defending Debbie against her father's unfair demands. Debbie's therapist sought to make a connection between her shoplifting and her frustrations with her parents. This helped Debbie understand her feelings of emotional deprivation as the root of her urge to steal. Gaining this insight, however, did not put an end to Debbie's kleptomania. Instead, when Debbie's father refused to continue paying for therapy—forcing Debbie to finance it herself—she began to steal department store items whose value equaled the cost of a therapy session. When the therapist asked Debbie to return the items, she refused. She continued to steal after each therapy session. Eventually the therapist stopped working with Debbie.

■　　　　■　　　　■

Disorders such as kleptomania have many causes, and their treatment is not always simple. The individual's past experiences and current environment play a role in triggering the compulsive need to steal. Biochemical imbalances may also contribute to the disorder. Determining the most effective treatment for each individual's unique manifestation of the disorder takes patience and perseverance. Perhaps most important, as with all the disorders discussed in this book, the sufferer must truly want to change.

The insanity defense has sometimes been used for kleptomaniacs who are brought to trial. Although juries, such as the one in this courtroom, rarely accept this plea, judges sometimes consider the defense when pronouncing sentence.

KLEPTOMANIA AND THE LAW

Since kleptomania is defined medically as an irresistible urge to steal, the question arises whether women such as Anne and Debbie should be held criminally responsible for their behavior. The so-called M'Naughten rule, formulated in England in 1843, stated that defendants cannot be convicted of a crime if they are incapable of realizing that a criminal act is wrong. People with kleptomania know that theft is wrong, however. They simply can't stop themselves from stealing without help.

In 1984 the Comprehensive Crime Control Act established that a defendant would not be held accountable for federal crimes committed if mental illness prevented him or her from appreciating the wrongful-ness of the act. However, the law also states, "Mental disease or defect does not otherwise constitute a defense" (Model Penal Code 402 98 Statute at 2057). This ruling means that accused individuals cannot claim innocence simply because they couldn't stop themselves from committing a crime. In other words, people suffering from kleptomania cannot escape the legal consequences of their actions.

People with impulse-control disorders such as kleptomania have not fared well using an insanity defense in the courts. Juries tend to take the view that, since the person is aware of his or her medical condition, it is the individual's responsibility to arrange for treatment or take other precautions to keep from stealing. Moreover, juries commonly perceive the impulse as "*not* resisted" rather than "irresistible." Nevertheless, diminished mental capacity can be a mitigating factor in sentencing. When an individual suffering from kleptomania is convicted of theft, the judge may be asked to show leniency. New findings that show that some people are able to resist stealing for the first time when they are properly medicated may cause us to rethink our entire sense of free will when it comes to diseases such as kleptomania.

Pyromania is the pathological fascination with and need to set fires. Although pyromania typically begins in childhood, not all juvenile fire setting is considered pyromania. In some cases, the behavior may be merely fire play, and in others it can be connected with delinquency and similar problems.

4

PYROMANIA—
THE COMPULSIVE NEED
TO SET FIRES

ourteen-year-old Jason is fascinated with fire. He lives with his mother, but he spends a lot of time alone because his mother is often so sick that she is confined to her bedroom. He never knew his father, who left the family before Jason's birth. Jason is angry with his mother for leaving him alone so often, and he is angry with his father for abandoning the family.

Jason has been setting small fires around the house since before his fourth birthday. This always succeeded in getting his mother's attention. Maybe, at first, this was part of the cause of Jason's interest in fire.

When Jason was 13, he played a game of "dare" with some other boys, in an abandoned field next to his home. Using a magnifying glass, he successfully reflected the sun's rays onto the dry grass, causing it to ignite. The following summer, Jason used a lighter to start a fire in an empty barn, which burned to the ground. Jason was ordered by juvenile court to spend six months in a residential home for juvenile offenders. Unfortunately, cigarettes and matches were accessible in the home, and Jason managed to start several small fires within his first six weeks in residence. Eventually, he set a large fire in the home's gymnasium, and he was sent back to juvenile court.

Jason's behavior is caused by a disorder known as pyromania. This pathological need to set fires involves multiple, deliberate attempts at fire setting that provide the arsonist (a person who willfully burns property) with a sense of psychological gratification and relief. People who suffer from pyromania are fascinated by fire and may be attracted to related paraphernalia—fire trucks, hoses, hydrants, and firefighters. Individuals with this disorder may seek to observe fires, set off false alarms, or associate themselves with fire departments. They do not set fires to make money, support a political ideology, conceal criminal activity, express anger or vengeance, improve their living situation, or respond to a delusion or hallucination. In other words, pyromania is not involved if an individual sets a fire to collect insurance money on a

It is common for pyromaniacs to be attracted to fire-fighting equipment, such as the fire truck, ladders, hoses, and protective gear shown here.

property, if a terrorist ignites a public building, if a criminal burns down a house to conceal a murder, or if angry rioters set businesses ablaze.

The diagnosis of pyromania cannot apply if a person sets fires because he or she is mentally retarded, is intoxicated with drugs or alcohol, or suffers from impaired judgment brought on by a medical condition. Neither can the diagnosis of pyromania apply if the individual sets fires because he or she suffers from another psychological disorder, such as the mistaken belief that nothing bad can come from his or her behavior or a schizophrenic disorder that has caused the person to lose touch with reality. A patient who believes he is the Messiah and has been commanded to burn down buildings, for instance, is not a pyromaniac.

PROFILE OF A PYROMANIAC

An individual who suffers from pyromania may spend a lot of time preparing for the fires that he or she sets. Frequently, the person is indifferent to the loss of life and property that fire setting causes. The individual may even derive pleasure from contemplating the resulting destruction, legal consequences, and danger to people's lives.

The *DSM-IV* specifies that pyromania is not a result of anger or vengeance. However, in *Impulsivity and Compulsivity*, Oldham, Hollander, and Skodol point out that, although these feelings may not be *consciously felt*, they are present subconsciously. In other words, the individual may truly *feel* no angry emotions that spur him or her to ignite a fire. Yet Oldham and colleagues report that they rarely work for any length of time with a pyromanic patient without discovering "not so far beneath the surface, enormous pools of vengeful feelings and rage."

Typically, pyromania begins in childhood. Although fire setting is a major problem in children (according to the *DSM-IV*, more than 40 percent of the people arrested for arson in the United States are under the age of 18), not all fire setting by children is considered pyromania. In fact, pyromania among children appears to be rare. Juvenile fire setting is usually associated with delinquency, conduct disorders, ADHD, and adjustment disorder (a stress-related disturbance characterized by marked distress in response to an identifiable stressor). Pyromania occurs much more often in males than in females, especially in males with poor social skills and learning difficulties. Overall, however, the disorder is rare.

Pyromania's course may wax and wane—considerable time may separate one fire-setting episode from the next. It is not known what percentage of children who set fires go on to become pyromaniacs. Youngsters sometimes play with matches and light fires as part of a developmental stage that involves experimentation. Such behavior does not constitute pyromania.

Some individuals with other mental disorders use fire setting as a way to communicate. They may wish to express hostility toward an institution where they are receiving treatment or convey a desire, a need for attention, or a sense of desperation. Such behavior is called "communicative arson" and although the physical results can be just as terrible, the problem should not be confused with pyromania.

As with other impulse-control disorders, the pyromaniac experiences

Pyromaniacs typically derive pleasure from setting and observing fires, and unlike individuals with kleptomania, they spend a significant amount of time planning their actions. They may even experience some thrill from contemplating the destruction that they will cause.

tension or arousal before the act, gratification or relief while committing it, and a general fascination or curiosity toward the object of his or her desire—fire. Because the individual typically derives great pleasure from being close to fires and their aftermath, he or she will often stay in the vicinity of the crime, even though it increases the chance of being apprehended.

CASE STUDY OF AN ADULT FIRE SETTER

James was raised in a family where no abuse was present. His mother died in a car accident when he was 12 years old, and, soon after, James began setting fires. From the beginning, he kept a detailed journal, recording each of his fires. He seemed to feel no remorse for his actions. James also set fire to a number of cats. But he showed no signs of psychosis or hallucination. Throughout his adult life, James has been in and out of jail on arson charges. He continues to show no sense of guilt for his crimes, and psychotherapy has done little to alleviate the problem.

STUDIES OF YOUNG FIRE SETTERS

Do young fire setters always go on to a life of pyromania as James did? A number of studies have been done in an effort to predict whether juvenile fire setters face a greater risk of developing pyromania later in life than does the general population. To find the answer to a question like this, scientists must conduct longitudinal studies—research that covers a long period of time, even spanning generations.

A research project by David J. Kolko and Alan E. Kazdin, described in their article "Children's Descriptions of Their Firesetting Incidents," revealed that, even though pyromania is present in only a small percentage of adult fire setting, "a childhood interest in fire is the most robust predictor of adult arson." The children in this study, who set fires mostly on other people's property, explained that they were "playing around" and that they lit the fires out of "curiosity" or "to have fun." A quarter of the children said they didn't know why they set the fires. They did not commonly give anger or revenge as a reason for their behavior. Half of the children acknowledged some forethought with regard to the activity, but fewer than half said that they planned how the fire would be set. Half reported a neutral or positive reaction to the incident. A small proportion of the children admitted that they would consider setting another fire. A quarter of the parents and nearly all the siblings of the youngsters were completely unaware that a fire had been set.

FIRE PLAY VERSUS FIRE SETTING

Fire Play (Childhood Experimentation)

1. The incident occurred only once.
2. The action was unplanned and spur-of-the-moment.
3. The subject burned paper, trash, or leaves.
4. The individual burned garbage or his or her own property.
5. The subject went for help or called the fire department.

Fire Setting (Pyromaniac Behavior)

1. The behavior has recurred.
2. The action was planned.
3. The subject used flammable or combustible material (for example, cooking oil or gasoline) to ignite property of some value.
4. The individual burned someone else's property, an animal, or a person.
5. The subject ran away.

Repeated episodes of fire setting were four times more likely among children who had a plan to light fires and who experienced a neutral or positive feeling after the first fire. An absence of parental reaction also increased the risk of future fire setting.

CASE HISTORIES OF YOUNG FIRE SETTERS

ALLEN

Allen is an eight-year-old boy who lives with his mother, stepfather, seventeen-year-old brother, and five-year-old sister. Allen's stepfather, who works in a factory, leaves for work each day at 2:30 in the afternoon and doesn't return until nearly midnight, long after Allen is asleep. Allen's mother waitresses during the dinner hour at a restaurant less than a block away from their home.

Because of their work schedules, both parents are usually out of the house during the after-school hours. During their absence, Allen's older brother supervises the two younger children. Allen's mother has been working under the assumption that, because her job is so close to the house, she will be able to handle any problems that arise. But Allen reports that his older brother regularly "beats him up." Allen's brother, who claims that Allen "drives him crazy," has recently admitted this physical abuse to social workers.

When Allen was five years old, his mother began finding used matchbooks in his pockets. When she questioned him about them, Allen claimed that he had picked up the matchbooks, already partially used, from the street. Recently, however, Allen's stepfather found him in his older brother's closet, using a candle to burn off the sleeves of his brother's shirts. Since then, Allen's brother has reported seeing Allen set numerous small fires in garbage cans and in piles of grass in the back-

Setting fire to someone's else's property is one of the characteristics that distinguish fire setting from fire play.

yard. School officials also informed Allen's parents that he is suspected of lighting a fire in the boys' restroom. Allen's parents took him in for therapy when he used lighter fluid to ignite his sister's bed.

DAMON

Damon is a thirteen-year-old who has been lighting fires since age six. Until recently, he lived with his parents and an older sister in her twenties. Damon's father and sister are seldom at home because of work responsibilities, but his mother is a full-time homemaker. Damon's mother reports that he has always been impulsive and excitable and that he frequently has temper tantrums when he's frustrated. Damon's problems have occupied most of her time.

At age six, Damon lit his first fire in his bedroom wastebasket. Then he began to set small fires in his backyard. The backyard fires became a regular occurrence, but since they were small and easily extinguished, Damon's mother was not seriously concerned.

Then, at age 10, Damon began lighting fires in school wastepaper receptacles. The school took immediate, and repeated, disciplinary action against Damon, but the behavior did not stop. When Damon was 11, he was referred to the school psychologist for evaluation and counseling. At the psychologist's recommendation, Damon was enrolled in the Big Brother program, and his fire setting subsided for nearly eight months. Three months ago, however, Damon's "big brother" moved, and Damon refused to meet with his new "big brother."

Last month, Damon lit two fires, one in a cemetery and one in a church. The fire department was called to extinguish the church fire, and legal action was taken. Damon is currently in a detention center awaiting trial in juvenile court.

CAUSES OF PYROMANIA

As with all impulse-control disorders, the relationship between biochemistry and psychology resembles the proverbial question: which came first, the chicken or the egg? Do people who suffer from pyromania have a biochemical disorder that accounts for their behavior—or do psychological traumas trigger this abnormal activity that, in turn, expresses itself in altered biochemistry? Although the issue of origins alludes us for now, ongoing research may give us new insights in the future.

One of the most promising lines of inquiry involves the issue of sensation seeking. As we discussed with regard to the connection between pathological gambling and thrill seeking (see chapter 2), a strong attraction to risk taking and other stimulating experiences may represent a compensation for inherent biochemical or genetic abnormalities. More and more research, in fact, points in this direction.

These findings offer hope in terms of treatment for and understanding of various mental disorders. It is possible that many of the disorders discussed in this book (as well as other illnesses) have a physiological origin that is aggravated by environmental factors. For instance, if a child inherits certain biochemical imbalances and is raised in an abusive or neglectful family, the youngster's genetic makeup combined with his or her environment may encourage the appearance of disorders such as pyromania. Neurochemistry affects a person's perception of reality and the way he or she relates to the outside world. And if distortion in perception is encouraged by an individual's surroundings, then disorders such as pyromania are more likely to appear.

TREATMENT

Since more and more research indicates a connection between biochemistry and the cause of pyromania, the disorder may respond best to drug therapy that corrects the biochemical imbalance. In *The Psychology of Child Firesetting*, however, authors Jessica Gaynor and Chris Hatcher claim that treatment is more effective if the problem is addressed in childhood than if intervention does not occur until adulthood. When working with a child who shows signs of pyromania, Gaynor and Hatcher recommend a combination of reeducation, family therapy, and behavior modification.

Early researchers approached this disorder from a purely psychoanalytic perspective. In other words, they tried to use counseling and emotional insights to redirect people with pyromania. In the article "A Primer on Pyromania," however, Drs. M. Mavromatis and J. R. Lion admit that "treatment for fire setters has been traditionally problematic due to the frequent refusal to take responsibility for the act, the use of denial, the existence of alcoholism, and the lack of insight." As with the other disorders discussed in this book, it is essential for the sufferer to acknowledge the problem before it can be addressed.

According to *The American Psychiatric Press Textbook on Psychiatry*, recovery is difficult when pyromania is associated with alcoholism or when a pattern of ritualized behaviors has been incorporated into the

Twelve-year-old Malcolm Shabazz, shown here leaving family court, pled guilty to setting a fire that fatally injured his grandmother. A psychologist testified that Shabazz had a history of fire setting that began at age three.

fire setting. In most cases, however, research indicates that people with this disorder respond to treatment and do not commonly have relapses. Frequently, pyromania lasts only a few years or during a specific period of a person's life. It often appears for the first time during a crisis and disappears when the crisis is resolved. People who have the ability to talk through their frustrations are apt to find a way to overcome this disorder.

PYROMANIA AND THE LAW

As with kleptomania, since pyromania is a mental disorder, the "insanity defense" has been used against criminal charges, but it has had a mixed history within the U.S. system of jurisprudence. (See the discussion under "Kleptomania and the Law" in chapter 3.) Only a very small proportion of arsonists suffer from pyromania, and obviously the possibilities for abusing this legal defense are enormous. Nevertheless, the concept of justice presumes free will. If a person is truly powerless to control his behavior, treatment rather than punishment is the more appropriate response.

We are all concerned about our appearance. This is no less true for people who suffer from trichotillomania. Even so, however, individuals with this disorder cannot keep from pulling out their own hair.

5

TRICHOTILLOMANIA AND SIMILAR PROBLEMS

J udy has an embarrassing habit: she can't seem to stop pulling out her hair. Whenever she's watching television or doing her homework, she finds herself pulling out strand after strand. If she's upset about something, she'll soon find her floor covered with long, dark hairs. She hates herself for doing this, especially since she longs to have thick, beautiful hair like her older sister, but the more she tries to stop herself, the more tense she feels—and the more tense she feels, the stronger is her urge to pull out her hair. Once she gives in and begins to pull, she feels a little better.

Judy's mother has told her this is a disgusting habit, and she reprimands Judy whenever she sees her pulling at her hair. Judy tries hard now not to pull her hair when anyone might see her. But recently she was horrified to notice that she has a patch on the side of her head that is nearly bald. She combs her hair over the spot now and hopes that no one will notice.

CHARACTERISTICS OF TRICHOTILLOMANIA

Trichotillomania is the name for Judy's compulsive hair pulling. The disorder is characterized by the recurrent pulling out of one's own hair, resulting in noticeable hair loss. A person with trichotillomania may pull out hair from any location on the body. Hair pulling may take place during periods of relaxation or distraction. The activity decreases stress, relieves tension, and is experienced as pleasurable by the person who suffers from this disorder. The individual may also fiddle with his or her hair in various ways. Although the resulting hair loss can be embarrassing, the sufferer feels unable to stop the behavior. The person may also pull other fibrous material in a similar manner. Nail biting, scratching, or gnawing are sometimes related to this affliction.

Although hair can be removed from any area of the body, the most common sites are the scalp, eyebrows, and eyelashes. Hair pulling may take place in brief episodes throughout the day or during less-frequent periods that can last

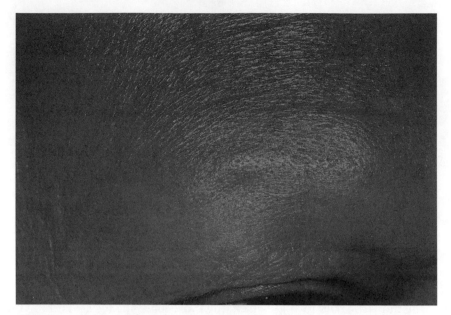

Trichotillomania can involve hair pulling from any area of the body. Hair loss is most often evidenced, however, on the scalp, the eyelashes, and (as shown here) the eyebrows.

for hours. Stressful circumstances may increase the amount of time spent pulling hair, but hair pulling may also take place when the person is watching television, reading a book, or otherwise concentrating on a separate activity. Tension typically rises before hair pulling and increases with attempts to resist the urge. A feeling of gratification accompanies the behavior. For some individuals an itching sensation prompts the hair pulling. The disorder causes sufferers considerable distress, including social problems and difficulties at work.

Examining the hair root, twirling the root off, putting the strand of hair between the teeth or under the fingernails, and eating the hair can accompany trichotillomania. People with this disorder don't usually pull out their hair in the presence of people other than close family members. Therefore, they may avoid social situations. They often deny the behavior or seek to conceal the resulting baldness or bald spots. Some individuals have urges to pull out other people's hairs and may try to find opportunities to do so surreptitiously. They may also pull hair from dolls, sweaters, or carpets. According to two studies, by researchers G. Christenson and colleagues and S. E. Swedo and colleagues, people with trichotillomania are more likely than the general population to suffer from mood and anxiety disorders or have histories of drug abuse.

Examining the hair that remains may reveal wrinkling of the outer root sheath or other signs of trauma to the follicles. The lack of inflammation of the scalp or other areas where hair once grew distinguishes this illness from baldness caused by various medical conditions. People with this disorder do not report experiencing pain from the hair pulling, and their patterns of hair loss can vary. Areas of complete baldness are common, as is noticeable thinned hair density. Sometimes, complete baldness is broken by hair at the nape of the neck or in a narrow perimeter around the outer margins of the scalp. Some individuals also pull hair from the limbs or torso. Eating hair may lead a sufferer to develop hair balls that can contribute to anemia, abdominal pain, nausea and vomiting, or bowel obstruction.

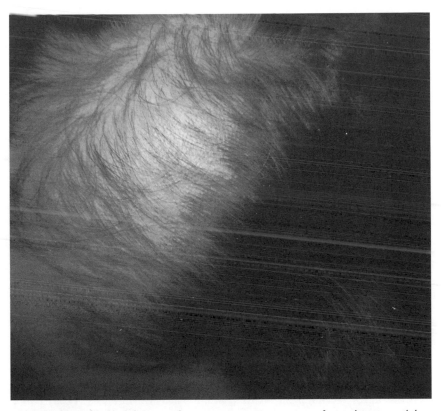

Although patterns of hair loss vary from person to person, areas of complete or partial baldness, such as this one, are typical.

Some researchers, including Dr. Swedo and colleagues, believe that trichotillomania is a compulsive behavior rather than an impulse-control disorder. Compulsive behaviors are recurrent—people with *obsessive-compulsive disorder* repeat the same behaviors over and over, and the behaviors often follow a pattern, a ritual that must be performed again and again. People who seek treatment for trichotillomania often do so for reasons that parallel those of people with obsessive-compulsive disorders—because of the shame and distress that they experience as a result of their inability to stop the behavior.

Trichotillomania is, however, different from obsessive-compulsive disorder in the following ways:

1. Trichotillomania is not purposeful or intentional.
2. It is not performed in response to an obsessional thought.
3. People with trichotillomania do not pull hair as a ritual to prevent some dreaded event or situation.
4. People with trichotillomania only pull hair, whereas most people with obsessive-compulsive disorder perform a variety of changing rituals.
5. Trichotillomania is predominately a female disorder, whereas equal percentages of women and men suffer from obsessive-compulsive disorder.

WHO SUFFERS FROM TRICHOTILLOMANIA?

Although men or women can develop this disorder, it appears to be much more common among women. Previously, experts thought that trichotillomania was less common than is now believed. According to the *DSM-IV*, recent surveys of college samples suggest that 1 to 2 percent of students have a current or past history of this illness.

Although trichotillomania usually begins in childhood, short periods of hair pulling during childhood may be constitute a benign habit that does not persist into adolescence or adulthood. Many patients who seek treatment for trichotillomania as adults report that they began between ages five and eight or around age thirteen. Some individuals experience continuous symptoms for decades. For others, the disorder can go into remission for weeks, months, or years. Periods of high stress may cause the condition to reappear. Hair pulling that is caused by another medical or psychiatric disorder should not be diagnosed as trichotillomania.

Many people manipulate their hair when they are under stress. This does not necessarily indicate trichotillomania. This young girl, for example, repeatedly runs her fingers through her hair to relieve tension.

Because hair pulling appears odd and irrational, the sufferer and other family members may be reluctant to speak about the problem to physicians or therapists. Because the public is generally not familiar with the disorder, the person who suffers from it may believe that no one else shares the problem. Once an individual with this disorder learns that he or she is not the only sufferer, attention can switch from the symptom to a cure.

Many people play with their hair, twist it, or otherwise manipulate it—particularly during times of stress. Some patients pull out their hair, but the hair loss is so slight that it's unnoticeable. A minimum of several months of such behavior, considerable hair loss, difficulty stopping the behavior, pleasure during hair pulling, and distress to the individual must all be present for trichotillomania to be diagnosed.

CASE HISTORIES

NANCY

Nancy, a 26-year-old woman, pulled several hundred hairs daily from her scalp, using only her left hand. She used brown hair spray to disguise the bald spots, and she supplemented the remaining hair with hair extensions. She pulled faster when she was stressed or depressed, but she pulled mostly when she was relaxed. The behavior started at age eight, when Nancy began carefully pulling out three hairs at a time.

In therapy, Nancy was treated with antidepressants and antianxiety drugs. She also received weekly behavior modification and counseling. After four months, she was pulling out only about 40 hairs per day. Her hair grew in enough that she no longer had to conceal her bald spots.

JACKIE

Jackie, a happily married mother of three children, showed up one day at the office of Dr. Judith Rapoport after seeing a documentary on the television show *20/20* about the doctor's successes treating obsessive-compulsive disorder with the drug clomipramine. Dr. Rapoport was conducting a clinical study at the National Institutes of Health, where she administered the drug to adolescents. Other doctors had also experienced great success using the drug to treat adults with obsessive-compulsive disorder. When Dr. Rapoport explained to Jackie that trichotillomania was an impulse-control disorder rather than an obsessive-compulsive disorder, Jackie disagreed and begged to be included in Dr. Rapoport's treatment. "I know it's crazy to pull out my hair," she said. "And I can't help doing it. I started when I was a kid. I kept it secret. You've got to let me be in your study."

Ever since Jackie was 13 years old, she had been pulling out her hair. Her grandmother claimed that it had started as Jackie's way of getting the attention of her mother, who was immersed in social activities of her own. Jackie didn't know whether this was the reason that she had started the behavior. All she knew was that she pulled out her hair and ate the roots. And she wanted to stop. "Can someone be an eyelash and hair *junkie?*" she asked Dr. Rapoport.

Jackie described the course her disease had taken. She had tried all sorts of maneuvers to keep herself from pulling out her hair: she had worn gloves, she had cut the ends of her fingers, she had clipped her fingernails so short that they bled. But nothing worked. She had to wear a wig and false eyelashes to hide her habit from the rest of the world. When she went swimming or was caught in the wind, she was always afraid that her wig and eyelashes would come off. According to Judy, "It was a crazy, awful adolescence."

When Jackie came to Dr. Rapoport's office, she wore a wide-brimmed straw hat to cover her wig and oversized mirrored sunglasses to hide her drawn-on eyebrows and her false eyelashes. Dr. Rapoport decided to include Jackie in the study because she had one truly obsessional symptom: whenever she pulled out hair, she had to make the results even. If she plucked two hairs from the right, she had to follow by plucking two hairs from the left.

Within a few weeks of starting to take clomipramine, a curious thing happened to Jackie. She still had an urge to pull out her hair; however, for the first time since she was a teenager, she was able to resist the urge. Two months later, Jackie came into the office wearing regular glasses. Her eyebrows and eyelashes had grown back. The hair on her head had also begun to grow. Dr. Rapoport described Jackie as "a new person," adding, "She bubbles."

MYTHOLOGY OF HAIR

In the Bible, when Samson's hair was cut, he lost his strength. In an interpretation of the fairy tale "Rapunzel," put forth by psychoanalyst Edith Buxbaum, hair represents separation and loss of the mother. Most psychoanalytic views of the meaning of cutting hair include loss of power, strength, or sexuality. In various Hindu cults and Christian monasteries, shaving the scalp is associated with mourning or penance. Especially among African Americans, head shaving has become a style associated with virile basketball players. For skinheads, head shaving symbolizes racism and anti-Semitism.

But none of this information explains why Jackie—who had no sexual problems, no hatred of racial groups, and no castration complex—couldn't stop pulling out her hair until she took a particular medication. Then the problem disappeared like magic.

Hair grooming rituals, such as the braiding that is about to begin in this illustration, are an important part of virtually every culture. Researchers have theorized that some such rituals are rooted in earlier instinctive animal grooming behaviors, which have simply gone awry in people with trichotillomania.

POSSIBLE CAUSES OF TRICHOTILLOMANIA

Some scientists hypothesize that hair pulling may hark back to grooming rituals that are "hard-wired" in animals—but in trichotillomania the programming has apparently gone haywire. Pruning feathers, licking to clean fur, or picking bugs and parasites off the animal's own fur or that of another animal are all forms of grooming that play a social role among animal groups. Animals perform these activities instinctively, and the behaviors are beneficial, so the relationship between this healthy animal activity and human disorders is unclear.

Dr. Rapoport comments on the many patients she treated who were suffering from trichotillomania: "Talking to these women, all so amazingly alike, gave me the eerie sense that a primitive behavior pattern had come loose. An innate, atavistic urge to groom, to preen, that can't be suppressed. The dramatic response of these hair pullers to [specific drug therapy] forges another link between this odd problem and obsessions and compulsions."

The response to drug therapy has caused many researchers to question whether trichotillomania is a form of obsessive-compulsive disorder rather than an impulse-control disorder. Would other so-called impulse-control disorders respond to the same drug therapy? The answer seems to be yes.

RELATED DISORDERS

It is not known whether trichotillomania is related to similar problems, such as compulsive lip biting or gnawing at the inside of the mouth, pathological pimple squeezing, compulsive scratching (in the absence of an itch), compulsive squeezing of the nose and other such gestures, and compulsive patting of the hair or other hair manipulation (such as beard stroking). The disorder may also be related to the compulsive sucking of blankets and other objects that can be rolled up into thin, hair-like projections and inserted into the nose, mouth, or other body cavities. People who practice these behaviors derive pleasure from them and have difficulty stopping them, in spite of the embarrassment that they cause.

People with intermittent explosive disorder typically explode in anger and violence in situations that do not merit the severity of their reactions. Here a young boy kicks a fan of an opposing soccer team.

INTERMITTENT EXPLOSIVE DISORDER

T he littlest things make Tom angry. All it takes is for someone to drive too slowly in front of him, and Tom blows his stack. If he finds a stain on his favorite shirt, or has to wait in line at the grocery store, or doesn't like his mother's tone of voice when she asks him to clean up his room—any or all of these situations can cause Tom to lose control. And once he's in a rage, it's best to stay out of his way. Tom can be pretty scary when he's angry.

After he explodes, Tom can't explain what got into him. He's ashamed and sorry, and, if his friends see him getting too angry over something insignificant, he feels embarrassed. His girlfriend broke up with him because she couldn't take his fits of rage, his friends have started to avoid him, and his school has expelled him twice for inappropriate conduct.

Last week, Tom found himself in even worse trouble. He got into a fight with another student in the school parking lot, and he ended up smashing his fist through the boy's car window. The school authorities called the police, and now Tom is facing legal charges.

Tom's problem is known as intermittent explosive disorder—a condition characterized by poor impulse control, which involves gross outbursts of rage (expressed verbally or through physical aggression) that provide a way for the person to vent anger and frustration. People with this disorder are considered excitable, aggressive, or overly responsive to environmental pressures. Their explosions are more intense than "normal" anger, and they cannot control them.

The underlying source of rage may sometimes be important relationships that were troubled and thus undermined the person's feelings of self-worth. The individual may then try to correct or "undo" this lingering sense of rejection by quickly forming other intense relationships. Great expectations are frequently followed by severe disappointments. A feeling of rage seems to be

For a person who has intermittent explosive disorder, the littlest annoyances can cause a blowup. This teenager, like Tom, explodes simply because he doesn't care for the tone of his mother's voice.

constantly floating somewhere inside the person, and the smallest setback can trigger it.

In the landmark book *The Impulsive Personality*, Dr. Wishnie describes life-and-death struggles over a book of matches, a place in line, and a game of pool—all of which he witnessed among hospitalized patients and prison inmates. For people suffering from explosive disorder, no issue is too trivial to precipitate a fight. Feeling a sense of failure and deprivation, these individuals lash out at the first sign of provocation. Wishnie cites the following case by way of example:

> Bill, a short man, was leaning against a Ping-Pong table. He was asked to move by Wendell, an extremely tall, muscular individual. Bill, sensitive about his size, thought he detected an insult in Wendell's voice. While Bill knew he was in the way, he refused to

move and challenged Wendell to move him. The two were stopped just short of a fight. At a minimum, both risked leaving the hospital and returning to prison; at a maximum [they risked] death, for each acknowledged that he had been prepared to kill the other. Bill later explained in group: "I'm nothing, but it would kill me to let those suckers know it. I've gotta show them all the time. It would just kill me if they knew. Then I'd really be nothing."

In his book *Violence*, Harvard professor James Gilligan offers a recent interpretation of Wishnie's research. According to Gilligan, shame and fear, combined with poor impulse control, cause most violent crime.

CHARACTERISTICS OF INTERMITTENT EXPLOSIVE DISORDER

Intermittent explosive disorder is characterized by the failure to resist episodes of aggressive impulses, which result in serious assaults or destruction of property. The degree of anger and violence displayed during such outbursts is entirely out of proportion with the incidents that provoked them.

For a diagnosis of intermittent explosive disorder to apply, the outbursts cannot be precipitated by other disorders or by medication. However, according to Oldham, Hollander, and Skodol's *Impulsivity and Compulsivity*, people with intermittent explosive disorder are almost always substance abusers as well. Research indicates that a relationship may also exist between ADHD and this disorder.

Individuals who suffer from intermittent explosive disorder are more apt to be male than female. They sometimes describe these eruptions of rage as "spells" or "attacks." Afterward, they may feel regret, remorse, or embarrassment. General aggressiveness or impulsivity may be evident between attacks. Under stress, individuals with other personality disorders may also be susceptible to such episodes of explosive rage. The disorder can cause job loss, suspension from school, divorce, accidents, difficulty with interpersonal relationships, hospitalization, or incarceration.

Nonspecific findings during neuropsychological testing—provided by an *electroencephalograph* (EEG), a machine that traces brain waves—show that patients with this disorder display evidence of abnormalities. Researchers have found signs of altered metabolism in the spinal fluid of some impulsive, temper-prone individuals, but the specific relationship of this physiology to the disorder is not yet clear.

Intermittent explosive disorder seems to begin anywhere from late adolescence to the third decade of life. Onset may be abrupt. Angry outbursts may also be associated with substance abuse and withdrawal from alcohol or drugs—particularly phencyclidine, cocaine, and other stimulants, inhalants, and barbiturates.

People who cause destruction for a specific purpose do not suffer from intermittent explosive disorder. That is, if a person uses violence to accomplish a particular goal, as is generally the case with terrorist acts, it is not an example of intermittent explosive disorder. Moreover, isolated acts are not typical of this disorder. Multiple outbreaks must occur in order for this diagnosis to apply.

In Southeast Asia, murderous ravings followed by amnesia are called

A scuffle that results from a single incident, such as this fender bender, does not necessarily indicate intermittent explosive disorder. For this diagnosis to apply, episodes of rage must be recurrent.

FEG readings have shown a number of abnormalities in the brains of patients with intermittent explosive disorder. The electrodes attached to this man's scalp detect the electrical impulses produced by his brain's activity. The impulses are then displayed as graphs on the monitor's screen.

amok. Similar episodes have also been reported in the United States and Canada. However, this condition generally involves only one incident rather than a pattern of behavior. And people who "run amok" typically forget what happened during their acts of rage. In intermittent explosive disorder, this is not commonly the case.

CASE STUDIES

MRS. BROWN

Mrs. Brown is a 35-year-old married woman with three children. Her husband sought marriage counseling when he became concerned about his wife's bursts of anger. As a result of Mrs. Brown's rage, she had become an abusive mother. Her children now feared her. Trivial occurrences brought on her anger—the smallest frustrations or the slightest change of plans. When one of her daughters came home late from a school event, for example, Mrs. Brown pulled out a hunk of the child's hair.

Therapy was hindered by the fact that Mrs. Brown became offended whenever the counselor pointed out that her behavior was harmful to her family. Each time the therapist tried to confront her about her behavior, Mrs. Brown responded with an angry outburst. Eventually, Mrs. Brown abandoned therapy altogether.

ALEX

In an article in the *American Journal of Psychiatry*, Drs. Ralph and Lucas Ryback describe the case of Alex, a 13-year-old boy who had been hospitalized many times in connection with his aggressive, belligerent behavior. He had a history of temper tantrums, screaming fits, violence toward others, social difficulties, argumentation, mood swings, depression, and difficulty paying attention in class. When Alex was frustrated or angered by other children, he would push, hit, and kick. Alex's mother lived in terror of her son's outbursts. Although Alex's conduct improved somewhat during the fourth grade, he seemed more depressed.

A year before Alex was evaluated, he had sustained a head injury that was followed by insomnia. To help Alex sleep, his doctors prescribed an oral drug. However, the medication did nothing to curb Alex's aggression. Although Alex's head trauma may have caused some mild neurological problems, he clearly suffered from intermittent explosive disorder before he was ever injured. Testing revealed that Alex also exhibited ADHD. He had difficulty remembering things, especially when comprehension of verbal material was involved, and he processed information very slowly.

During the previous school year, Alex had stopped doing homework, and his grades had dropped. During his evaluation, Alex admitted that he felt angry. He confessed that he had smashed household items and had thrown a rock through a car window.

Over the years, Alex's doctors gave him a series of different medications, none of which helped control his behavior. Eventually, however, they achieved some success with a combination of Alex's sleep medication and a drug designed to correct an imbalance in the chemicals that transfer messages between nerves. They gradually increased the medication over a four-day period until they reached the correct dosage.

The frequency and intensity of Alex's explosive episodes began to decrease—even when he was provoked. His temperament became calmer, and he was now able to accept constructive criticism from his mother and from his teachers.

During the next four months, Alex was able to control his temper and experienced only minor episodes of irritation. When Alex became angry, his teachers could direct his attention elsewhere. Alex's mother was overjoyed and described the change in her son as nothing short of a miracle.

GEORGE

George is a 47-year-old lawyer who repeatedly "loses his cool" at work. Recently, he even punched out another member of the firm. His angry outbursts have cost him many a friend and girlfriend.

When George sought counseling, he seemed to respond readily to psychotherapy. He quickly gained insight into the connection between his anger and his abusive childhood. However, his outbursts continued unchecked.

Behavior modification proved unsuccessful for George, and drugs designed to correct imbalances of serotonin in the brain gave him severe headaches. At last, however, he began to see results from the ongoing emotional support from his therapist. Whenever he felt the impulse to get angry, he would call his therapist and talk out his feelings. George also began to take low doses of an antidepressant medication. Although his symptoms never totally disappeared, he gradually achieved greater control of his anger.

DISCUSSION OF TREATMENTS

These studies—and others like them—demonstrate that terms such as *aggression* and *impulsivity* refer to more than merely vague psychological states. They may actually reflect biochemical abnormalities that can be measured with relative precision. Although some people may be tempted to think that individuals with illnesses such as intermittent explosive disorder are not really sick but simply need to "shape up," recent studies indicate that biochemical abnormalities cause many destructive behaviors.

As we saw in the case of Alex, changes in conduct may involve more than good parenting and supportive teachers. In fact, medication can go a long way toward relieving the physiological problems that underlie such disorders. For people like Alex's mother, who did her best to control her son to no avail, the possibility of a biochemical cause brings new hope for a cure. Even so—as evidenced in the cases of Mrs. Brown and

Violent actions that are committed for a specific purpose are not indicative of intermittent explosive disorder. These rival gang members, for example, are involved in a turf war.

George—medication is not always the answer. Each person's problems and needs must be addressed individually.

CONCLUSION

Medication offers hope to people who suffer from impulse-control disorders. Many of the people who suffer from these disorders who have been helped by drug therapy could neither understand nor control their compulsions before medication changed the nature of their world. Although other therapies are valuable as well, they often work best when combined with drug therapy. In the past, we have tended to separate our emotions from our physiology, but it is becoming increasingly clear that our bodies and our minds make up one being.

In some cases, the symptoms of impulse-control disorders may never completely disappear. But it is important to remember that mental disorders exist on a spectrum that ranges from completely "normal" behavior to behavior that controls and limits a person's ability to live out his or her life. Accordingly, treatment can be considered successful when a person is able to resume normal function with a minimum of anxiety and distress.

APPENDIX

FOR MORE INFORMATION

American Psychiatric Association
1400 K Street NW
Washington, DC 20005
(202) 682-6000
http://www.psych.org/

**American Psychological Association
(APA)**
750 First Street NE
Washington, DC 20002
(202) 336-5500
http://www.apa.org/

**Cleptomaniacs and Shoplifters
Anonymous (CASA)**
512 E. Huron
Ann Arbor, MI 48104
(313) 913-6990

Gamblers Anonymous
P.O. Box 17173
Los Angeles, CA 90017
(213) 386-8789

Knowledge Exchange Network (KEN)
Center for Mental Health Services
P.O. Box 42490
Washington, DC 20015
(800) 789-2647
E-mail: ken@mentalhealth.org
http://www.mentalhealth.org/

National Council on Problem Gambling
445 W. 59th Street
New York, NY 10019
(212) 765-3833
(800) 522-4700

**National Institute of Mental Health
(NIMH)**
NIMH Public Inquiries
6001 Executive Boulevard
Room 8184, MSC 9663
Bethesda, MD 20892-9663
(301) 443-4513
E-mail: nimhinfo@nih.gov
http://www.nimh.nih.gov/

**National Mental Health Association
(NMHA)**
1021 Prince Street
Alexandria, VA 22314-2971
(703) 684-7722
(800) 969-6642
http://www.nmha.org/

APPENDIX

BIBLIOGRAPHY

American Psychiatric Association. *Diagnostic and Statistical Manual of Mental Disorders.* 4th ed. Washington, D.C.: American Psychiatric Association, 1994.

Berman, Linda, and Mary-Ellen Siegel. *Behind the 8-Ball.* New York: Simon and Schuster, 1992.

Brenner, Reuven, with Gariella A. Brenner. *Gambling and Speculation: A Theory, a History, and a Future of Some Human Decisions.* New York: Cambridge University Press, 1990.

Christenson, G., T. B. MacKenzie, and J. E. Mitchell. "Characteristics of 60 Adult Chronic Hair Pullers." *American Journal of Psychiatry* 148 (1991): 365–70.

Dostoyevsky, Fyodor. *The Gambler.* New York: E. P. Dutton, 1915.

Feeney, Daniel, and William Klykylo. "Treatment for Kleptomania." *Journal of the American Academy of Child and Adolescent Psychiatry* 36, no. 6 (1997): 723–24.

Gaynor, Jessica, and Chris Hatcher. *The Psychology of Child Firesetting.* New York: Brunner/Mazel, 1987.

Gilligan, James. *Violence: Reflections on a National Epidemic.* New York: Vintage, 1997.

Griffiths, Mark. *Adolescent Gambling.* New York: Routledge, 1995.

Hales, Robert E., Stuart C. Yudofsky, and John A. Talbott, eds. *The American Psychiatric Press Textbook of Psychiatry.* 3rd ed. Washington, D.C.: American Psychiatric Press, 1999.

Hodgson, R., and S. Rachman. "Obsessional Compulsive Complaints." *Behavioral Research Therapy* 15 (1987): 389–95.

Kallick, Maureen, et al. *A Survey of American Gambling Attitudes and Behavior.* Ann Arbor: University of Michigan Institute for Social Research, 1979.

Kolko, David J., and Alan E. Kazdin. "Children's Descriptions of their Fire-setting Incidents: Characteristics and Relationship to Recidivism." *Journal of the American Academy of Child and Adolescent Psychiatry* (January 1994): 32–57.

Legg, R. Charles, and David Booth, eds. "Young People and Fruit Machine Gambling." In *Appetite: Natural and Behavioral Bases.* New York: Oxford University Press, 1994.

Lepkifer, E., et al. "The Treatment of Kleptomania with Serotonin Reuptake Inhibitors." *Clinical Neuropharmacology* 22, no. 1 (1999): 40–43.

Mavromatis, M., and J. R. Lion. "A Primer on Pyromania." *Diseases of the Nervous System* 38 (1977): 954–55.

McCormick, R. A., and J. I. Taber. "The Pathological Gambler: Salient Personality Variables." In *Handbook on Pathologic Gambling*, ed. T. Galiski. Springfield, Ill.: Charles C Thomas, 1987.

Munting, Roger. *An Economic and Social History of Gambling in Britain and the USA.* New York: Manchester University Press, 1996.

Oldham, John M., Eric Hollander, and Andrew E. Skodol, eds. *Impulsivity and Compulsivity.* Washington, D.C.: American Psychiatric Press, 1996.

Rapoport, Judith L. *The Boy Who Couldn't Stop Washing: The Experience and Treatment of Obsessive-Compulsive Disorder.* New York: E. P. Dutton, 1989.

Ratey, John, and Catherine Johnson. *Shadow Syndromes.* New York: Pantheon, 1997.

Riconda, Andrew, ed. *Gambling.* New York: H. W. Wilson, 1995.

Ryback, Ralph, and Lucas Ryback. "Gabapentin for Behavioral Dyscontrol." *American Journal of Psychiatry* (September 1995).

Shaffer, Howard J., et al., eds. *Compulsive Gambling: Theory, Research, and Practice.* Lexington, Mass.: Lexington Books, 1989.

Shaw, George Bernard. *Man and Superman.* New York: Heritage Press, 1962.

Sternlieb, George, and James W. Hughes. *The Atlantic City Gamble.* Cambridge, Mass.: Harvard University Press, 1983.

Swedo, S. E., et al. "A Double-Blind Comparison of Clomipramine and Desipramine in the Treatment of Trichotillomania." *New England Journal of Medicine* 321 (1989): 497–501.

Swedo, S. E., and E. Hollander, eds. *Trichotillomania in Obsessive-Compulsive Related Disorders.* Washington, D.C.: American Psychiatric Press, 1999.

Wagenaar, Willern Albert. *Paradoxes of Gambling Behavior.* Hillsdale, N.J.: Lawrence Erlbaum Associates, 1988.

Walker, Michael B. *The Psychology of Gambling.* New York: Pergamon Press, 1992.

Wishnie, Howard. *The Impulsive Personality: Understanding People with Destructive Character Disorders.* New York: Plenum Press, 1979.

Zuckerman, Marvin, ed. *Biological Bases of Sensation Seeking, Impulsivity, and Anxiety.* Hillsdale, N.J.: Lawrence Erlbaum Associates, 1983.

APPENDIX

FURTHER READING

Berman, Linda, and Mary-Ellen Siegel. *Behind the 8-Ball.* New York: Simon and Schuster, 1992.

Gaynor, Jessica, and Chris Hatcher. *The Psychology of Child Firesetting.* New York: Brunner/Mazel, 1987.

Gilligan, James. *Violence: Reflections on a National Epidemic.* New York: Vintage, 1997.

Griffiths, Mark. *Adolescent Gambling.* New York: Routledge, 1995.

Hollander, Eric, ed. *Trichotillomania in Obsessive-Compulsive Related Disorders.* Washington, D.C.: American Psychiatric Press, 1999.

Munting, Roger. *An Economic and Social History of Gambling in Britain and the USA.* New York: Manchester University Press, 1996.

Oldham, John M., Eric Hollander, and Andrew E. Skodol, eds. *Impulsivity and Compulsivity.* Washington, D.C.: American Psychiatric Press, 1996.

Rapoport, Judith L. *The Boy Who Couldn't Stop Washing: The Experience and Treatment of Obsessive-Compulsive Disorder.* New York: E. P. Dutton, 1989.

Ratey, John, and Catherine Johnson. *Shadow Syndromes.* New York: Pantheon, 1997.

Riconda, Andrew, ed. *Gambling.* New York: H. W. Wilson, 1995.

Walker, Michael B. *The Psychology of Gambling.* New York: Pergamon Press, 1992.

Addiction: a compulsive need for a substance or activity that is known to be harmful.

Antidepressants: a group of medications, of several different chemical types, often used to relieve or prevent feelings of depression.

Attention-deficit disorder: a set of learning and behavior problems that interfere with a person's ability to pay attention. Impulsive behaviors usually play a part in this disorder. It is often accompanied by *hyperactivity* (see below).

Behavior modification: a form of therapy that uses reinforcement techniques to teach desirable behaviors and eliminate undesirable behaviors.

Bipolar disorder: a mood disorder in which manic (excited) states alternate with depressed states.

Chronic: persisting for a very long time.

Codependency: a condition in which someone is controlled or manipulated by an addicted individual, usually a spouse or close family member.

Compulsion: the psychological need to repeat a behavior over and over.

Dysfunctional: unhealthy.

Ego-dystonic: describes behavior by an individual that goes against the person's own sense of what is right.

Electroencephalograph (EEG): a machine that traces brain waves.

Enabler: A person who makes it easier for another individual's undesirable behavior to continue—by making excuses for it or helping to hide it, for example.

Hyperactivity: a condition in which individuals are abnormally active. People with this condition often feel incapable of being still.

Maladaptive: describes behavior that makes a person's life more difficult.

Mania: an excited state in which a person feels agitated and restless. The person may also have irrational beliefs of grandeur and power.

Narcissism: a selfish, egocentric love of oneself.

Obsessive-compulsive disorder: a condition characterized by recurrent obsessions (persistent thoughts or ideas) or compulsions (repetitive, ritualistic behaviors) that are time-consuming or distressful and that significantly impair a person's life.

Pathological: abnormal.

Psychotherapy: "talk" therapy, in which a patient and therapist discuss the patient's feelings, behaviors, and problems and how to change them in desirable ways.

Serotonin: a chemical in the body that allows messages to be passed from nerve to nerve.

APPENDIX

INDEX

ADD. *See* Attention-deficit disorder

Addiction, 34, 35

ADHD. *See* Attention-deficit/ hyperactivity disorder

Adjustment disorder, 55

Age
    and intermittent explosive disorder, 78
    and pathological gambling, 33
    and pyromania, 57
    and trichotillomania, 68

Aggression, 81

Alcohol abuse, 14, 33, 35, 63

Alcoholics Anonymous, 35, 48

American Journal of Psychiatry, 44–45, 80

American Psychiatric Press Textbook of Psychiatry, 44–45, 63

Amok, 79

Antidepressants, 35

Antisocial personality, 14, 33

Anxiety disorders, 43, 67

"A Primer on Pyromania" (Mavromatis and Lion), 61

Attention-deficit disorder (ADD), 33

Attention-deficit/hyperactivity disorder (ADHD), 33, 55
    and intermittent explosive disorder, 77, 80

Behavior modification, 36

Behind the 8-Ball (Berman and Siegel), 31–32

Berman, Dr. Linda, 31, 32

Bipolar disorder, 35, 48, 49

Burstein, Dr. A., 47

Buxbaum, Edith, 72

CASA. *See* Cleptomaniacs and Shoplifters Anonymous

Children, 38, 57–60
    and pyromania, 61

"Children's Descriptions of Their Firesetting Incidents" (Kolko and Kazdin), 57

Christenson, G., 66

Chronic, 15

Cleptomaniacs and Shoplifters Anonymous (CASA), 47–48

Clomipramine, 70, 71

Codependency, 37

Communicative arson, 55

Comprehensive Crime Control Act, 50–51

Compulsion, 15

Conduct disorders, 14, 57

Diagnostic and Statistical Manual of Mental Disorders (DSM-IV), 9, 13, 20
    and kleptomania, 43
    and pathological gambling, 25, 30, 33, 34
    and pyromania, 57
    and trichotillomania, 68

Drug abuse. *See* Substance abuse

Dysfunctional, 38

Eating disorders, 43
EEG. *See* Electroencephalograph
Ego-dystonic, 43
Electroencephalograph (EEG), 77
Electrotherapy, 47
Enabler, 37

GA. *See* Gamblers Anonymous
Gam-Anon, 35
Gam-Ateen, 35
Gamblers Anonymous (GA), 33,
    35–36, 48
Gambling
    and big business, 27, 29–30
    as cultural phenomenon,
        25–26
    historical origins of, 26–27,
        29–30
    pathological (*see* Pathological
        gambling)
Gaynor, Jessica, 61
Gender
    and intermittent explosive dis-
        order, 77
    and kleptomania, 43, 45
    and pathological gambling, 33,
        43
    and pyromania, 57
    and trichotillomania, 68
Gilligan, James, 77
Goldman, M. J., 45

Hair, 71, 72
Handbook on Pathologic Gambling
    (McCormick and Taber), 35
Hatcher, Chris, 61
Hollander, Eric, 47, 57, 77
Hyperactivity, 33

Impulse, 11
Impulse-control disorders, 9,
    11–12, 13
    characteristics of, 15–22
    treatment for, 9, 16, 22–23

Impulsive Personality, The (Wish-
    nie), 17, 18, 76–77
Impulsivity, 9, 12, 81
    and other mental disorders,
        12–13, 14
Impulsivity and Compulsivity (Old-
    ham, Hollander and Skodol),
    47, 57, 77
Intermittent explosive disorder, 14,
    75–77
    case studies of, 79–81
    causes of, 81–82
    characteristics of, 77–79
    treatment for, 81–83

Johnson, Catherine, 11, 18

Kazdin, Alan E., 57
Kleptomania, 14, 21, 41–45
    case histories of, 48–49
    and the law, 50–51, 63
    treatment for, 23, 47, 49
Kolko, David J., 57

Lamarr, Hedy, 44
Lepkifer, E., 47
Lion, J. R., 61

Mania, 35
Maladaptive, 15
Mavromatis, Dr. M., 61
McCormick, R. A., 35
McElroy, S. L., 45
Medication, 9, 81–82
Mental disorders
    causes of, 14
    classifications of, 14–15
    and impulse-control disorders,
        14, 33
    and impulsivity, 11–12
Money, 30, 32
Mood disorders
    and impulse-control disorders,
        14, 33, 43, 67

Narcissism, 33
National Council on Compulsive
    Gambling, 27
Native American reservations, 29

Obsessive-compulsive disorder
    and trichotillomania, 68, 70, 73
Oldham, John M., 47, 57, 77

Pathological, 9
Pathological gambling, 14, 30–33,
    61
    as addiction, 34–35
    causes of, 33, 35
    and professional or social
        gambling, 33–34
    treatment for, 23, 35–36
    treatment for families of,
        37–39
Poor impulse control. See impulse-
    control disorders
Psychology of Child Firesetting
    (Gaynor and Hatcher), 61
Psychotherapy, 14, 47
Pyromania, 14, 53–54
    case studies of, 57, 58–60
    causes of, 60–61
    and the law, 63
    profile of, 55, 57
    treatment for, 23, 61, 63

Rapoport, Dr. Judith, 70–71, 73
Ratey, Dr. John, 11, 18
Ryback, Drs. Ralph and Lucas, 80

Schizophrenia, 14
Serotonin, 47, 81

Shadow Syndromes (Ratey and
    Johnson), 11–12, 18
Siegel, Mary-Ellen, 31, 32
Skodol, Andrew E., 47, 57, 77
Substance abuse
    and compulsive gambling, 33,
        35
    and impulse-control disorders,
        14, 17
    and intermittent explosive dis-
        order, 77, 78
    and trichotillomania, 67
    See also Alcohol abuse
Swedo, S. E., 66, 68

Taber, J. I., 35
Treatment
    for families of pathological
        gamblers, 37–39
    for impulse-control disorders,
        9, 16, 22–23
    for intermittent explosive dis-
        order, 81–83
    for kleptomania, 23, 47, 49
    for pathological gambling, 23,
        35–36
    for pyromania, 23, 61, 63
    for trichotillomania, 73
Trichotillomania, 14, 65–68
    case histories of, 70–71
    causes of, 72–73
    diagnosis of, 68–70
    and related disorders, 73
    treatment for, 73

Violence (Gilligan), 77

Wishnie, Dr. Howard, 17, 18, 76–77

APPENDIX

PICTURE CREDITS

page

8: © Paul Viant/FPG International LLC

10: © Shirley Zeiberg/Photo Researchers

13: © Richard Hutchings/Photo Researchers

22: © Barbara Rios/Photo Researchers

23: © Will and Deni McIntyre, Science Source/Photo Researchers

24: Archive Photos/Lambert

28: Reuters/Joe Tarver/Archive Photos

29: AP/Wide World Photos

31: Photofest

34: © Jerry Wachter/Photo Researchers

37: © Richard T. Nowitz/Photo Researchers

40: © Richard Hutchings/Photo Researchers

42: © Bob Combs/Photo Researchers

45: AP/Wide World Photos

46: © Blair Seitz/Photo Researchers

48: © Will McIntyre, Science Source/Photo Researchers

50: © Ron Chapple/Photo Researchers

52: Will Hui/Image Bank, 1997

54: AP/Wide World Photos

56: AP/Wide World Photos

59: AP/Wide World Photos

62: AP/Wide World Photos

64: John Banagan/Image Bank, 1996

66: © Dr. P. Marazzi, Science Source/Photo Researchers

67: © J. F. Wilson/Photo Researchers

69: © Telegraph Colour Library/FPG International LLC

72: Mercury Archives/Image Bank, 1994

74: AP/Wide World Photos

76: © Richard Hutchings/Photo Researchers

78: © Paul Sequiera/Photo Researchers

79: Deep Light Productions, Science Photo Library/Photo Researchers

82: AP/Wide World Photos

Senior Consulting Editor Carol C. Nadelson, M.D., is president and chief executive officer of the American Psychiatric Press, Inc., staff physician at Cambridge Hospital, and Clinical Professor of Psychiatry at Harvard Medical School. In addition to her work with the American Psychiatric Association, which she served as vice president in 1981–83 and president in 1985–86, Dr. Nadelson has been actively involved in other major psychiatric organizations, including the Group for the Advancement of Psychiatry, the American College of Psychiatrists, the Association for Academic Psychiatry, the American Association of Directors of Psychiatric Residency Training Programs, the American Psychosomatic Society, and the American College of Mental Health Administrators. In addition, she has been a consultant to the Psychiatric Education Branch of the National Institute of Mental Health and has served on the editorial boards of several journals. Doctor Nadelson has received many awards, including the Gold Medal Award for significant and ongoing contributions in the field of psychiatry, the Elizabeth Blackwell Award for contributions to the causes of women in medicine, and the Distinguished Service Award from the American College of Psychiatrists for outstanding achievements and leadership in the field of psychiatry.

Consulting Editor Claire E. Reinburg, M.A., is editorial director of the American Psychiatric Press, Inc., which publishes about 60 new books and six journals a year. She is a graduate of Georgetown University in Washington, D.C., where she earned bachelor of arts and master of arts degrees in English. She is a member of the Council of Biology Editors, the Women's National Book Association, the Society for Scholarly Publishing, and Washington Book Publishers.

Linda Bayer, Ph.D., graduated from Boston University and received a master's degree in English and a doctorate in humanities from Clark University. She later earned a master's degree in psychology from Harvard University. She worked with patients suffering from substance abuse and other problems at a guidance center and in the Boston public school system. Bayer was also a high school teacher before joining the faculties of several universities, including Wesleyan University, Hartford College for Women, American University, Boston University, and the U.S. Naval Academy. At the Hebrew University in Israel, she occupied the Sam and Ayala Zacks Chair. Bayer has also worked as a newspaper editor and a syndicated columnist, winning a Simon Rockower Award for excellence in journalism. Her published works include *The Gothic Imagination, The Blessing and the Curse* (a novel), and several books on substance abuse, as well as five volumes in the ENCYCLOPEDIA OF PSYCHOLOGICAL DISORDERS. Bayer is currently a senior speechwriter and a strategic analyst at the White House. She is the mother of two children, Lev and Ilana.